We Can Reclaim
Our Errant Youth

To The Lady who
keeps me beautiful
BeBe Garcia
with appreciation

a. d. Schepps

We Can Reclaim Our Errant Youth

A. I. Schepps

VANTAGE PRESS
New York

FIRST EDITION

All rights reserved, including the right of
reproduction in whole or in part in any form.

Copyright © 1996 by A. I. Schepps

Published by Vantage Press, Inc.
516 West 34th Street, New York, New York 10001

Manufactured in the United States of America
ISBN: 0-533-11833-6

Library of Congress Catalog Card No.: 95-91047

0 9 8 7 6 5 4 3 2 1

Contents

Preface

The deteriorating conduct of many of our nation's young people has deeply concerned me for years. In response, during the past few years I have read every article relevant to this subject that has come to my attention. And now I have written this book, which, I believe, effectively addresses the troubles of our youth and will, if its advice be followed, turn them to the ways that have healthfully sustained the people of our country for over two hundred years. The educational system that I propose will inculcate in our children the values of morality, respect for others, respect for oneself, a sound work ethic, and self-dependence. The lack of these values are the deficiencies that, I believe, are afflicting our young people today.

Looking back, I wish to compliment the many reporters in the media who do such a good job informing our citizens of what is happening in our country. Without their informative reports, I would never have attempted this venture. They have not only reported events; they have also picked the brains of individuals from all areas of our law enforcement and legal systems, including judges, prosecuting attorneys, police officers, jailers, juvenile authorities, and prison officials. These reporters have not even been averse to going into the ghettoes and getting, first-hand, the sad stories of what goes on in the minds of young killers.

I should also like to commend and thank all the publishers of newspapers and magazines who provide a forum for news of the sort that is cited in the following chapters. I have learned much regarding the deterioration of our youth from publications of many kinds, even picking up some good information in newspapers in Scotland, Ireland, Wales, and England during two trips to Europe in 1994. I found that England, too, is having some problems among her youth similar to those found in the United States.

From the time I prepared my manuscripts and the time this book went into production, much time elapsed. Actually, my preparation for this publication was cut off December, 1995. Therefore, I hope my readers will understand if some of my statements may not be up to date by the time the book is published.

Finally, I wish to thank my daughter Nancy Brand for all the typing and retyping of the chapters that follow. I promised her, and she is expecting, a new set of fingers.

We Can Reclaim
Our Errant Youth

CHAPTER 1

Our Unguided and Out-of-Control Youth

Since 1960 the population of our country increased 41 percent. Within 30 years, violent crime increased 560 percent. Illegitimate births increased 400 percent. Divorces quadrupled. Children living with single parents tripled. Teenage suicides increased 200 percent. SAT scores dropped 80 points. Modern pathologies, at least great parts of them, have gotten worse. They seem impervious to government spending on their alleviation, even very large amounts of spending.

Although the Great Society experienced some successes, there is a growing body of evidence which indicates its remedies have, in many cases, reached their limits. Many of the most serious social and behavioral problems we now face (particularly among our young) are remarkable resistant to governmental cures. How intelligently and honestly we address problems is the critical social policy question of the decade.

—William J. Bennett, 1993

As America approaches the twenty-first century, we as a nation are in disarray over problems that continue to grow ever more perplexing. As we consider the breakdown of the nuclear family, the use of drugs, youth violence, and other issues, it is plain that many of these problems concern and impact upon our young people.

More than any other industrial country, the United States is experiencing deterioration in the character of

1

its youth—and this condition is worsening. There are areas of our country where up to 60 percent of our youth have had brushes with the police. These combined with crimes committed by adults, render the loss of life and property in America the highest of any civilized country. The threat of crime has reached the point today that it is even frightening would-be visitors from foreign countries from traveling to the United States.

Every day we read in our newspapers and magazines articles concerning the moral decline of our young people. Crime committed by young hoodlums is on the increase. Gangs are recruiting members not yet in their teens. In addition, the advent of more and more children born to single mothers who are themselves children—unable to properly raise, much less control their offspring—is exacerbating this condition. Statisticians, health-care professionals, jurists, police, prison officials, reporters and commentators in the media, and others constantly relay to us the sordid deeds committed by misguided youth. Billions of dollars have been spent to correct the deteriorating lives of the many children who each year become statistics on police records. But nothing seems to really turn the problem around, and the moral and spiritual decay of our youth continues. We find ourselves mesmerized to the point at which we try to ignore this incessant bad news and hope not to hear any more about it. But this is not possible, for life goes on and the streets remain unsafe.

Parents are afraid to send their children to school, and many children who wish to learn fear going to school, for both inside and outside the schools, on the playground and in the classroom, gang members and dope dealers ply their trade. Even primary schools are targeted by dope dealers, who bribe children to do their dirty work for them. Too many of these children succumb to the big money that is paid them; a great many youths who wind up in prison experienced just such a beginning.

At one time, teachers controlled their classrooms. Until the era of World War II, parents were in accord with teachers for good deportment of schoolchildren. Sadly, such is no longer the case. In part because of the drug culture, schoolchildren smuggle weapons into school and use them on classmates. Understandably, because of the potential for violence or threats of lawsuits, teachers are intimidated and cannot teach effectively, spending much of their time simply trying to establish order. They often serve as mere caretakers, who plead with children to behave, working desperately in school systems that do not give them the necessary support to control the unruly. Teachers are frustrated, not only because there is so little they are authorized to do, but also because they get little cooperation from parents of miscreant children. The bad apples are that way because there is little or no discipline at home, with parents who are either absent or uncaring.

As this condition intensifies, the quality of our children's education, quite clearly, declines. And as alarming and discouraging as these facts are, I believe the worst comes after uninterested and troublesome students leave school. It is then that they turn, full time, to unlawful interests that to them are far more important than obtaining an education ever was. To them, school was just a place to meet like-minded types and to use as a launchpad to further lawlessness. The nation's prisons are full of these former students, now young adults given to robbery, rape, murder, and other crimes.

The many who leave school before getting a high-school education find themselves unable to get jobs that will support a family. Girls taste the adventure of womanhood too quickly, have babies, and thereby lessen their chances of enjoying their young lives to the fullest, much less escaping the drudgery of going it alone. The business world is demanding more and more education for workers applying for jobs. In the face of this, too many of our children do not even finish high school, and it seems—as noted above—that many parents do not care.

It is plain that the added millions of dollars spent by the federal and state governments over the past few years, designed to enhance the quality of education, have gone for naught. The number of law-enforcement officers has increased manyfold to keep up with the ever-increasing nefarious activities of our youth. Despite their best efforts, gangs are multiplying. Because of gang activity, our hospital emergency rooms are kept busy patching up the victims of lawlessness. The taxpayers, increasingly concerned, are picking up the greatest share of this cost.

Understandably, our elected leaders are in a quandary. Candidates for office seize upon the youth crime issue to campaign for tougher laws, finding this the ticket to election. Office holders try to remedy the condition with new laws, the hiring of more police, and the building of more prisons.

While the cost of doing so is enormous, the building of prisons is one of the fastest-growing industries in the United States, with all highly populated states today spending millions of dollars building more prisons. Along with this, sophisticated devices—electronic "leashes" and such—are being developed and employed to control or apprehend lawbreakers. Add to this the booming growth in antiburglary devices for homes and businesses, and we are no longer spending millions, but *billions* of dollars to defend ourselves from our own citizens.

The United States already has the highest percentage of its population behind bars of any nation in the industrialized world—about 1.5 million people, says Charles Thomas, professor at the University of Florida in Gainesville. And, according to a *Wall Street Journal/NBC News* poll, more than 70 percent of those surveyed support longer prison terms for violent offenders. Ironically, while ever-harsher punishment is meted out, we see few favorable results.

What has happened? Our children have come to see improper conduct as adventurous, romantic, thrilling, and challenging. Behavior deemed intolerable in an earlier day is now seen as acceptable and desirable. Unless these children have been well brought up and schooled from the first, they may well choose to follow the wrongful, destructive way. Children permitted too much freedom, with little moral upbringing from early childhood to early teenage years, may well reach a point later in life at which they are unable to turn back from that wrong road. At that point, no amount of police presence can prevent them from having a run-in with the law.

Consider for a moment American young people of 1940. For the most part, children had parents at home with them—or at least one parent at home with them. Parents knew what their children were doing. One-parent families were rare. Today, even in families where both the mother and father are present, in many instances both parents work outside the home in order to make a living. This, unfortunately, leaves children by themselves for many unsupervised hours. As a result, opportunities abound for today's children to take up with bad company and to get into serious trouble. This is especially true for one-parent families.

In a pertinent statement, former secretary of education, William J. Bennett, has written:

> A disturbing and telling sign of the declining condition among the young is the result of an on-going teacher survey. Over the years teachers have been asked to identify the top problems in America's public schools. In 1940, teachers identified talking out of turn; chewing gum; making noise; running in the halls; cutting in line; dress code infractions; and littering. When asked the same question in 1990, the teachers identified drug abuse; alcohol abuse; pregnancy; suicide; rape; robbery; and assault.

Children of the 1940s did not have televisions that were constantly blaring examples of hate, killing, rape, pornography, drug and alcohol consumption, profanity, and other such attitudes and acts at young minds. There is no doubt that these diabolical examples of depravity affect many minds. Children attend movies that have the same effect as do the television shows, even with the current rating system, which has failed in its purpose: to preclude certain films from children's view. Then there is the accessibility of pornographic sites on the Internet, which allows children to view the vilest filth imaginable.

As Bennett has written:

> This palpable cultural decline is the manifestation of a marked shift in the public's beliefs, attitudes and priorities. Social scientist James Q. Wilson writes that "the powers exercised by the institutions of social control have been constrained and people, especially young people, have embraced an ethos that values self-expression over self-control." According to pollster Daniel Yankelovich, "our society now places less value than before on what we owe others as a matter of moral obligation; less value on

sacrifice as a moral good; less value on social conformity, respectability, and observing the rules; and less value on correctness and restraint in matters of physical pleasure and sexuality. Higher value is now placed on things like self-expression, individualism, and personal choice."

To date there has not been an all-inclusive system devised to bring an effective end to this escalating problem. In succeeding chapters I will outline methods for changing this pattern. In my attempt to come up with an understanding of the cause of these problems and to arrive at a solution, I have attempted to read every report by knowledgeable people who have written on the subject. I will quote from many of these reports in the next chapter.

After my readers have digested what follows, I hope they will arrive at the same remedy I have, one which, if instituted, will in time return our youth to the norms and values that make for a civil culture.

Friends, in approximately one generation—thirty years—we have witnessed the greatest (and worst) transformation of the character of American youth in the nation's history, marked by a dramatic turn from proper behavior to destructive behavior. This should be considered the most damaging phenomenon that we have encountered during this century, not excluding the wars in which we have participated. I hope that what follows effectively solves the problem—and soon—for every day that passes brings the United States closer to disaster, in the form of complete social chaos.

CHAPTER 2
Front-Line Reports

The author has studied the deterioration of conduct among our youth for several years. The past three years have seen a prolific output in the number of reports on this subject written by media reporters, judges, policemen, prosecutors, juvenile department workers, educators, law breakers and others. These reports have been very enlightening and reflect accurately the causes and effects of what has brought about the deteriorating character of our youth and the resulting escalation in crime that our nation suffers. I have chosen what I consider a representative cross-section of such material, excerpted it, and inserted these items in this chapter, with the hope that my readers will read each one. Nearly all are poignant and depressing. Each time I read one of these items, I ask myself how this can be: how and why such a depressing situation can go on in our country. I believe that too many of us are so disturbed by such articles that when we see it in print we just glance over them, unable to stomach any more bad news. Nevertheless, this is our country, and it behooves us to address her problems and try to correct them.

I hope my readers will not only read all of these, but will also agree with the answers I advocate as solutions to the problems described herein.

In December 1993, Secretary of Housing and Urban Development (HUD) Henry Cisneros, speaking in Houston, said that unless something is done to curb the youth violence he fears what our country will be like by the year 2010. "Children grow up with no hope—our society would do well to inculcate religion . . . We are about to lose our current youth generation."

On January 2, 1994, on "Face the Nation," Bob Schieffer said 160,000 children stay home every day because they are afraid to go to school.

The September 19, 1994, *Time* magazine contains an article relative to juvenile delinquency, titled "When Kids Go Bad." It states that America's juvenile justice system is antiquated and no longer able to cope with the violence wrought by children whom no one would call innocents. The article details a number of terrible crimes committed by children 13 to 15 years of age. Society is sending such children for long terms to prison. Taxpayers will have to pay many dollars to incarcerate these people. When they get out, chances are they will be unable to find jobs to support themselves. It may well be that such people will have become hardened and want revenge on society. In that event, they will commit still more heinous crimes.

From *The Houston Chronicle* of September 13, 1994: The U.S. has next to the highest incarceration rate in the world. Only Russia with a rate of 558 per 100,000 is higher. The U.S. rate has jumped 22 percent since 1989. It now stands at 519 per 100,000. The reporting group, The Sentencing Project, which promotes alternative sentencing, concluded that get-tough policies of the past two decades have failed to reduce violent crime.

Four out of five teenage mothers end up in poverty.

Illegitimacy is now five-and-a-half times what it was 30 years ago. Nearly 30 percent of all live births are of children born to unmarried mothers. Illegitimacy accounts for 68 percent of all black births. In inner cities this reaches as high as 80 percent.

Two-thirds of all children held in detention are from fatherless homes.

According to a *Time* magazine article on February 7, 1994, close to one-fifth of all violent crime is committed by kids under 18 years of age. If not incarcerated, 60 percent of these will be rearrested for another crime within one year.

The kids who have gone wrong are looking for get-rich schemes.

Kids start out as drug offenders, go to property crime, and then commit crime against people. In prison, they learn bigger crime ways.

Jailing our way out has proved to be futile.

In the past two decades, we have spent $37 billion on new prisons and $5 billion more is on order.

In the past decade, our prison population has doubled to 925,000 and our jail population has tripled to 450,000. (In October 1994, it is reported our prison population has passed one million.)

On October 13, 1994, the Center for Disease Control at Atlanta reported that violence among our youth is increasing. The homicide rate among males 15 to 19 more than doubled from 1985 to 1991. The rise was attributed to gangs and guns. The homicide rate went from 13 per

100,000 to 33 per 100,000 of population. These homicides in 88 percent of the cases were attributed to guns.

In August 1993, the American Psychological Association released the result of a three-year study concluding that violence among youth can be reversed with appropriate programs.

"As psychologists we are convinced that aggression is primarily a learned behavior, and since it is learned it can be unlearned, or conditions can be set up so that it is not learned in the first place," said Leonard Eron, professor of psychology at the University of Michigan and chairman of a ten-member panel.

The report noted that violence has increased dramatically in the past 15 years. It attributed the increase to the large number of children growing up in poor and abusive households, easier access to guns, discrimination against various ethnic and racial groups, and the glamourization of violence in the media.

Item: "Why Prisons Don't Work," by Wilbert Rideau in *Time,* March 21, 1994.

Getting tough has always been a 'silver bullet,' a quick fix for the crime and violence that society fears. Each year in Louisiana—where excess is a way of life—lawmakers have tried to outdo each other in legislating harsher mandatory penalties and in reducing avenues of release. The only thing to do with criminals, they say, is get tougher. They have. In the process, the purpose of prison began to change. The state boasts one of the highest lockup rates in the country, imposes the most severe penalties in the nation, and vies to execute more criminals per capita than anywhere else. This state is so tough that last year, when prison authorities here wanted to punish an inmate in solitary confinement for an infraction, the most they could inflict on him was to deprive him of his underwear. It was all he had left.

If getting tough resulted in public safety, Louisiana citizens would be the safest in the nation. They're not. Louisiana has the highest murder rate among states.†

Columnist William Raspberry observed in one of his columns:

"You and I are guided by the belief that good things will happen to us in the future if we take proper care of the present. But without hope for the future, hard work for a low-paying job makes no sense. Working hard in school or pleasing a boss or avoiding pregnancy makes no sense.

"Of course, this makes no sense to us. But placed in the shoes of young people who have had no encouragement and hope it should become clear to us why children think this way."‡

The November 14, 1994 edition of *Time* carried an article that contrasts three-strike laws with early intervention in the life of a boy on the wrong road. The reporter Jill Smolowe interviews Sneakers, a 21-year-old gang member in Milwaukee. Sneakers explains he got that name because he is real fast. Sneakers has done three years for two robberies. He is not worried about a third felony. He explains, "The law don't make no difference to me because I ain't gonna get caught, I mean if I really thought I was gonna get caught, I wouldn't commit a crime in the first place, now would I." Smolowe also interviewed Iman Reed now 16. At 11, Iman liked to pick fights on the streets of Wichita, Kansas, making him a prime target for revenge shooting. His mom enrolled him in a Big Brother program, which paired him with a police detective. Now, Iman is pulling down A's and B's and has his sights on a law degree. Reflecting back, Iman concludes, "If I wasn't in the program I'd be in one of those gangs or I'd be dead."

On June 2, 1996, on the program *Meet the Press,* House Speaker Newt Gingrich, in his rapid style, spoke about our juvenile problem. This is my understanding of what he said: the issue we really have to deal with, far beyond entrepreneurship, is the survival of American civilization. No civilization can survive with twelve-year-olds having babies, fifteen-year-olds killing each other, seventeen-year-olds dying with AIDS, and eighteen-year-olds getting diplomas they can't read. And this is a genuine crisis of our civilization because we have everywhere in America these kinds of things happening at a growing rate in a way that means you can't transfer to the next generation the core habits and the core structures of being civilized.

In his column of January 2, 1995, William Raspberry tells of a visit made by Rev. Jesse Jackson to the Cook County Jail where he spoke to young black inmates. Excerpts of what Jackson said to the inmates appear below:

Today, our civil wrongs constitute the number one threat to our progress. The surrender to drugs, dropouts, and violence, the abandoned families and alienated children are not only eroding our base, they are also fueling the politics of fear, anger, and repression.

13

The power, three strikes and you're out is driven by you. The $24 billion crime bill is driven by you. Your behavior, or a fundamental change in your behavior, will determine much of America's future. You have the power.

How many of you have wives and children at home on welfare? Your child doesn't need welfare or an orphanage; your child needs a daddy and a mother at home. You have the power to change welfare.

You have the power to change violence and crime just by changing your mind. You have the power to change the gun market, the drug market, the family structure of America. You have the power to save our children.

There is a 75 percent recidivism rate in Cook County. If you can cut that back to 50 percent, you would change the criminal justice system.*

Indeed, we will all agree this is a powerful message and noble effort on the part of Rev. Jackson. The big problem is that the effort is late. Had those inmates been brought up properly, they would not be there.

Item: "Americans Feel Families and Values Are Eroding, But They Disagree Over the Causes and Solutions," by Gerald F. Seib in *The Wall Street Journal,* June 11, 1993.

Sharon Nutbrown is deeply worried about disintegrating families and declining values in America, and she thinks economic pressures are to blame. "A lot of it is that both parents have to work," says the Pennsylvania mother of two, a Democrat. "A lot of it is that kids are left home a lot."

Harold Peterson is equally convinced that families and values are deteriorating in America—but disagrees completely that economics is the root cause. "It's a decline

* 1995, Washington Post Writers Group. Reprinted with permission.

in morals," declares the Oklahoma father of four, a Republican. "Economics is an excuse."

Those two Americans neatly frame one of the country's most important trends. There appears to be a growing belief across the political spectrum that social values are eroding and that the decline of the family is at the heart of the problem. While there seems to be an emerging consensus on those fundamental points, though, there's little agreement on what to do about the problem or what government actions might help.*

"Getting the Boot Repeatedly: Recidivism High for Offenders in Programs, Study Shows," in *The Houston Chronicle,* April 13, 1994.

"Boot camp prison programs do not prevent their graduates from returning to prison for new crimes, a study released Tuesday by the University of Maryland found.

"Out of the eight states examined in the study—Florida, Georgia, Illinois, Louisiana, New York, Oklahoma, South Carolina and Texas—Georgia's boot camp prisoners had the highest rate of recidivism, while New York's had the lowest. The study, conducted by professor Doris MacKenzie, found that in all eight states, prisoners who had completed the boot camp program were equally as likely as offenders who spent longer periods of time in prison to commit new crimes."†

Item: "Never-Wed Parents Rise in Statistics," by Richard Whitmire in *The Houston Post,* July 20, 1994.

---

* Reprinted from *The Wall Street Journal,* June 11, 1993.
† Copyright 1994 Houston Chronicle Publishing Company. Reprinted with permission. All rights reserved.

"The Census Bureau has picked up a new twist to the trend of single parenthood in America: Nearly half the children involved were not the products of divorce, but were born out of wedlock.

"The result, according to the report released Tuesday, is a new class of single-parent families.

"Ten years ago, a child living with one parent was twice as likely to be the product of a broken home as to have been born out of wedlock. Now, 37 percent live with a divorced parent, 35 percent with a never-married parent. The balance have other living arrangements, such as foster homes or relatives. . . ."*

Item: "Violence Tightens Grip on Public Schools," by Tom Watson and Carol J. Castaneda in *The Houston Post,* June 10, 1993.

"Columbus, Ga.—Seven sixth-graders were doing more than math inside Georgetown Elementary School. Police said they were hatching plots to kill their teacher.

" 'If it wasn't so damn serious, it'd be hilarious,' Maj. John Wood said Wednesday. . . .

"Police said the botched attacks on Sherry James began two months ago because the kids thought she was too strict. 'She was making them behave all year and they didn't like that,' said sixth-grader Jeremy Owens."†

Item: "Study: U.S. Losing a Generation," by Richard Whitmire in *The Houston Post,* June 22, 1993.

"The problems of American youth have swelled into a 'human and national tragedy,' concludes a book-length report due out for release today by the National Research Council.

"Called *Losing Generations,* the research panel's report estimates 7 million young Americans, about one-fourth of all 10-to-17-year-olds, are at risk of failing to lead productive adult lives.

"The National Research Council is an arm of the National Academy of Sciences."*

Item: "No Options," by Helen Cooper in *The Wall Street Journal,* June 21, 1993.

"Eloise Garcia is a welfare statistic waiting to happen.

"Not that the 25-year-old single mother of three is on welfare. She isn't. In fact, she is thrilled with her new job as a clerical and computer assistant at a Dallas tax consultant's office—her first desk job ever.

"But consider: Ms. Garcia's $6-an-hour pay translates into $214 a week. Rent costs $300 a month. Utility bills, food and other essentials for a family of four quickly eat up the rest of the monthly take.

"All that is manageable, Ms. Garcia says. But in a couple of weeks, she will lose the six-month day-care stipend from a charitable agency that has allowed her to take her three children to a center every day. And unless Ms. Garcia finds another charity willing to foot the bill for her children's care, she will, in all likelihood, have to quit her job and head for the welfare rolls. There is no way she can afford the $692 monthly charge to put her three children in day care.

" 'I'm willing to go to the church, anywhere, to beg for help with day-care,' " Ms. Garcia says. " 'Tell me what to do. I really like my job. I don't want to leave. I've never worked in an office before.' "

Item: "Tolerance: For a Teacher, It Can Be Such a Frustrating and Harmful Word," by Rebecca Maitland in *The Houston Chronicle,* April 17, 1994.

I'm a teacher of history to high school students who really aren't interested in what happened in the past. Their greatest concern is what to wear on their date Friday night, why their boyfriend canceled their date for Thursday and who's the new girl in school about whom everyone is talking.

As I stood in front of my class one day talking about the Pilgrims and trying to explain that the word 'Pilgrims' means English Puritans, I walked the aisles taking up notes about new miniskirts and rapper pants. I gathered those notes without stopping my lecture on the Christian beliefs that molded this country, reading from the textbook: 'Americans shared a common heritage of Judeo-Christian teachings. These included the belief that individuals were responsible to God for their conduct and would be rewarded or punished in a life after death . . .'

Suddenly, I was interrupted.

A young boy, looking older than his years, stood up and told me I could not teach him anything about Christianity because, he said, it is against the law. He had on three earrings and a T-shirt that read, "Smoking Joe." For a moment I hesitated and didn't have an answer. I walked back to my desk and had a seat. All eyes were on me, the room was quiet, the note passing came to a halt.

My mind raced as I wondered if the Supreme Court justices would block out our true history for the sake of those who do not believe in God. I wondered if our Forefathers would be purged from the history books because people today believe in tolerance, of silence, of silencing beliefs. Then the question came to my mind: "Is the silencing of beliefs actually tolerance or is unbelief actually being supported?"

The young man was still standing, looking, staring at me. I asked him to be seated.

"Sir," I said, "I am not teaching you Christianity, I am teaching you history. History is full of people who believed in God, in protecting their country, and for standing up for a faith that built this nation. . . ."*

---

* Rebecca Smith Maitland. Copyright 1994 Houston Chronicle Publishing Company. Reprinted with permission. All rights reserved.

"Before I could finish, he jumped from his seat and said, 'My mother is on the committee to have all that Christian stuff taken out of the textbooks. We don't care what this country was founded on and we think it is stupid to even mention what the people believed, they should just put in the textbooks what happened, the facts, not beliefs.'"

Item: "Black Children Face Desperate Life Crises," by Cassandra Spratling in *The Houston Chronicle,* May 27, 1994.

" 'Black children are facing one of their worst crises since slavery,' children's advocate Marian Wright Edelman said Wednesday in announcing results of a national survey on the feelings, fears, and hopes of black adults and children.

" 'The poll confirms that the black child crisis, one of the worst since slavery, is real,' said Edelman, president of the Children's Defense Fund.

" 'The disturbing news is that this is just the tip of the American iceberg of pervasive child and family neglect, and the disintegration of spiritual, community and family values across race and class.' "*

Item: "Violent Youths Would as Soon Kill You as Look at You," by William Pack in *The Houston Post,* November 15, 1993.

"Houston and America are producing an alarming number of youths who show no concern for other individuals, can kill innocent victims without remorse and are

---

* Reprinted by permission: Tribune Media Services. Copyright 1994 Houston Chronicle Publishing Company. All rights reserved.

incapable of linking their actions with consequences, experts contend.

"The number, some agree, may even be growing."*

Item: "Big Stick Alone Can't Control Juvenile Criminals," by Donald Kaul in *The Houston Chronicle,* November 28, 1993.

Being against juvenile crime is easy. Doing something about it; that's hard. Each day brings us fresh stories of young people committing vicious, brutal crimes with a casualness that beggars the imagination. . . .

The most persuasive recent statement of the get-tough school was delivered by John Ray, a Washington, D.C., councilman, writing in the *Washington Post.*

He was responding to President Clinton's well-received speech in Memphis, where Clinton invoked the name of Martin Luther King Jr. in speaking about crime in the African-American community.

The President had said: "The freedom to die before you're a teenager is not what Martin Luther King lived and died for." He called for a reaching-out to black youth.

"We will take away their guns and give them hope."

That ticked Ray, a black man, off. He wrote:

"It is . . . time that we come to grips with the fact that the explosion of senseless violence that we are experiencing in our inner cities is not being fueled just by misguided children in need of an inspirational sermon and a job at the post office.

"In fact, we are seeing a resurgence of hard-core gangsterism the likes of which this country hasn't experienced since the days of Al Capone.

"These hoodlums aren't looking for a job. They have a job; they are full-time, swaggering criminals, and they are good at what they do. They sell drugs, run guns, rob and steal. They have no respect for human life and will kill you without provocation. Worst of all, they're getting away with it in increasing numbers, and their brazen behavior is becoming a role model for the next generation. . . .

"Mr. President, the thugs who are plying their deadly trade on America's streets don't deserve to be mentioned in the same breath as Dr. King. They deserve to be led to a jail cell, not to the promised land. We need to fight this war with the same force and intensity with which we fought Al Capone. . . . It is not an issue of race and culture. It is an issue of crime and punishment."

Those are the words of a man on the firing line of the urban wars and they carry the conviction not of prejudice but of desperation.*

Item: "Can Uncle Sam Ever Really Take Place of Mom and Dad?" by Richard Whitmire in *The Houston Post,* November 5, 1993.

"Where are the parents? Why aren't they turning off the TV, teaching manners, feeding breakfast, or making sure their children aren't carrying guns?

"The quick answer is both simple and perplexing. The rising number of fatherless families and working mothers—and especially the fact that more than one out of five American children live in poverty—means for a lot of children there's no parent around to turn off the TV."†

Item: "Schools Find Pregnancy Difficult Subject," by George Flynn in *The Houston Chronicle,* October 10, 1993.

21

Hempstead, Tex.—In the locker-lined hallway near Hempstead High School's front entrance hangs a stark remnant of happier times. Letters, carefully painted on a long strip of white butcher paper, list the teams, band, cheering squad and coaches.

"We are Family!" the banner proclaims.

But in recent days, the corridors have echoed with less-congenial sentiments as parents and educators have faced off in the school library, which also serves as the school board's meeting room.

The Hempstead Independent School District has been thrust into the national spotlight by the stormy debate that arose after revelations that four of the high school's 16 cheerleaders were pregnant.

A survey of some Houston-area school systems indicates, however, that such a dilemma would be no easier for officials outside Hempstead. Among them, there appears to be no uniform approach to the issues involved—or even firm answers about permissible activities for pregnant students and the prospective fathers.*

Item: "What Is Our Biggest Problem?" By James P. Gannon in *The Houston Post,* December 19, 1993.

"Chances are you have never heard of Charles Murray. He's a rather obscure social scientist typical of those who populate Washington think tanks. But with one stroke, Murray has propelled a provocative idea into the nation's debate over welfare.

"America's most serious social problem is not crime or drugs or poverty, but rather its soaring rate of illegitimate births, which breeds all those social ills, Murray contends. And the only way to deter illegitimacy is to attach an economic penalty to it: End welfare payments to unwed mothers."*

Item: "Hard-Core Rap Music Receiving a Bad Review From Many Blacks," by Michel Marriott, in *The Houston Chronicle,* August 15, 1993.

" 'People are outraged, man,' said the Rev. Calvin O. Butts III, pastor of the Abyssinian Baptist Church in Harlem who has taken up a crusade against hard-core rap. 'You get to the point where you are constantly hearing, over and over, talk about mugging people, killing women, beating women, sexual behavior. When young people see this—14, 15, 16 years of age—they think this is acceptable behavior.'

"Yet many rap performers casually dismiss the complaints about songs and videos that exalt the immediate gratifications of sexual conquests, remorseless violence and 'gangsta' values of materialism and self-interest. 'What is said is OK as long as they're paid for it,' said Dr. Dre, one of whose videos shows a young man yanking off the bikini top of a young woman playing volleyball."†

Item: "Parents of Many Students Are the Real Dropouts," by Thomas French in *The Houston Chronicle,* August 24, 1993.

"Whenever parents ask what's gone wrong with our public schools, my first instinct is to hand them a mirror. I go to a kindergarten in Pinellas County, Fla., where I

---

* Copyright 1993. USA TODAY. Reprinted with permission.
† Copyright © 1993 by The New York Times Co. Reprinted by Permission.

live and work, and meet a little boy who often walks around with a shell-shocked expression.

"This boy's home life is filled with turmoil: His mother and stepfather always seem to be fighting.

"Early one morning, after the stepfather shatters an ashtray against a wall, the child collects the shards and brings them to school. He clutches them to his chest, insisting to his teacher that he has to try to put everything back together."*

Item: "The Social Issue for '94: Revival of Fatherhood," by Don Eberly in *The Houston Chronicle,* January 3, 1994.

"Fathers play a unique and irreplaceable role in the nurture of children, particularly in restraining the impulses of adolescent males.

"Perhaps this is why President Clinton recently took to the pulpit once occupied by Martin Luther King Jr. to suggest that social progress will not be possible so long as fathers are free to abandon their children.

" 'Ending welfare as we know it,' as the president suggested, is a popular and commendable objective. But society should not indulge its desire to end the 'subsidization of illegitimacy' without acknowledging its culpability for the decline in social values across all races and classes, which has contributed equally to the problem."†

CHAPTER 3
Our Schools Today

America's colonists came from Europe holding a variety of attitudes toward education and its end. During the young nations's early years, many systems were tried in an effort to bring about a single system that would meet the educational needs of the colonists; indeed for several generations the various systems brought over from Europe were in competition. About 1860, a consensus of the best educational system for the United States began to coalesce. This consensus became a movement, which then became refined into our American system of public schooling, reflecting the condition of a democratic industrial civilization.

The rise of the public school has been inextricably tied to the rise of the modern United States, and this relationship continues to this day. The cause of one is invariably the cause of the other. I believe it is the duty of both teachers and lay citizens to promote public education, thereby enabling the United States to follow its early pattern and fulfill its destiny. The current disarray in our schools, described in chapter 1, must lead us to agree that the destiny of our schools and our nation hangs in the balance.

Because of the problems of our schools, we pour ever more dollars into our school system—extra dollars that do not seem to help. For higher education, more and more scholarships are being offered to those students who show seriousness of purpose. Still, industry is finding that high school graduates do not measure up to what is demanded in the working world. Even college graduates are found not to meet industry's entry-level standards.

Every day our newspapers contain many advertisements seeking qualified workers. While there is nearly always a high unemployment record in parts of this country, many jobs go wanting. This should be a great source of concern and compel us to seek answers. On a few related facts, we can readily agree. Many applicants are turned down because of poor or not enough schooling. Many are refused because of substance abuse. Many are refused because of a work history reflecting poor job performance. Many people do not apply because they do not want to work—a government handout is good enough. Many do not apply because there is good income in nefarious activity, such as stealing. Many do not apply because of a low starting salary, with poor advancement opportunities. (Indeed, some unemployed citizens would prefer to have no income rather than income they consider inadequate.) Many of these low-paying types of jobs are taken by illegal aliens, who feel blessed to obtain this or any other kind of work. Many jobs that go unfilled could be filled if only we turned out better qualified students.

Bill Mintz of *The Houston Chronicle* reports that a worker's education will determine his fate, noting that college-educated Americans earn almost twice as much as those with only high school diplomas. College graduates still enjoy virtually full employment and comprehensive benefits. The opposite is true of high school dropouts, whose jobless rates are almost four times higher. Most dropouts lucky enough to have jobs do not have health insurance through their employers.

Most Americans will not attend four-year universities, but even entry-level jobs require workers who can read, write, and compute: who can conceive, present, and manipulate information both intellectually and electronically. Continuing education is becoming almost mandatory, and community colleges will play an increasingly important role in the success of middle-class Americans. Throughout its history, America has been a land of opportunity for those willing to work. Young Americans today must be convinced of the fact that tomorrow's opportunities are being rapidly reserved for those willing to study and learn as well.

To accent the above, I recount the story of Thomas Williams, which appeared in *The Wall Street Journal,* March 11, 1994. Williams was a high school teacher. He left his teaching job at 43 years of age and took a job in an assembly plant of the Ford Motor Co. It was not long ago that Ford did not want educated people in their factories. Ford and Chrysler both have changed their focus in their hiring. During the next decade, they expect to hire over 75,000 workers. These workers will have to be highly motivated and highly educated. Mr. Williams made last year $50,000, more than twice what he made teaching.

The cost of educating tomorrow's workers is not cheap. An article in *The Houston Post* by Cal Thomas reports some figures on these costs. The U.S. Dept. Of Education reports that an average of $5,920 was spent on each pupil in public elementary and secondary schools in 1993 — a record. That is $200 per pupil more than was spent in 1992, and, adjusting for inflation marks, a 50 percent increase in spending on public education in the past decade.

Have the public schools produced a superior product for a higher price? Thomas says they have not. In fact, the reverse is true, with SAT scores down 75 points from where they were thirty years ago.

Secretary of Education Richard Riley touched on one reason for the decline of public education in his "An Open Letter to a Parent." Riley says parents must "slow down the pace of our lives to help our children grow." He adds that "education starts with values. . . . If a parent or a family member places value on integrity, a commitment to excellence and studying hard, children come to school prepared to learn. Parents create the frame, teachers help kids fill the picture."

Former Secretary of Education William Bennett has noted, "We desperately need to recover a sense of the fundamental purpose of education, which is to engage in the architecture of souls." Bennett also said, "It is almost as if we have been conducting an unwilling social experiment saying, 'Let's have children. Let's not raise them. Let's not teach them right values. Let's support them entirely on government. Let's see how they turn out.' Now, the results are in."

Industry throughout the world is getting more and more complicated. As I have shown, our schools are not keeping up. Upon completing school, students in other industrial countries are much better prepared than are our students to enter the job market. The United States could find itself relegated to a second-rate country if we do not bring our school system in consonance with our industry.

The learning of reading, writing, arithmetic, and other essentials for education is the primary purpose of our schools. As important as the 3 R's and other subjects are, they are no more important than are ethics. The diminution of these values is what drives down the ability of our teachers to teach and fosters the committing of crime by our children.

Much of the education in the thirteen colonies was parochial. A family that was void of religion and did not belong to any religious establishment was indeed rare. The colonists' books generally had religious content. In those days the standards of morality were not in dispute. Practically everyone recognized, adhered to, or at least paid lip-service to Judeo-Christian ethics. It was therefore a foregone conclusion that children in school were from law-abiding and upright homes. Teachers did not have to concern themselves with teaching morals.

As late as 1848, Horace Mann, Secretary of Education for the Commonwealth of Massachusetts, argued that the responsibility for formulating political and religious views was not that of the school, but of the parents. So it is no wonder that the Framers of our Constitution had no problem wording the first of our constitutional amendments. They all were certain the children of our schools would need no teaching in ethics, which were learned at home. With this foundation swept away, most enlightened citizens of our country readily agree that its fruit—the failure to inculcate morality in our children—is the greatest single factor afflicting our society today.

(While examining the Constitution and its implications for our children, I considered another amendment, the misapplication of which has brought and is bringing death to many of our children and adults. Of course, here I am referring to the Second Amendment and to that public nemesis, the handgun.

The Second Amendment reads, "A well regulated militia, being necessary to the security of a free state, the right of people to keep and bear arms, shall not be infringed." The clear intent of the Framers of our Constitution was to make sure that people who had muskets were permitted to keep them so that they could defend our country in time of need. The Framers still were not sure about the intentions of England or the Indians. There were few pistols in those days, and most certainly pistols were not used widely by soldiers in combat. Clearly, that amendment was to cover *muskets* with which to battle an enemy, not a small, hidden device for surprising and killing civilians. It was only at the time of the Civil War that pistols were introduced in small numbers to the Union and Confederate armies. John Adams, Ben Franklin, and all the other writers of our Constitution could not foresee that pistols would someday pervade our land and that in the hands of children such a weapon would become the detestable and murderous device that it is. Could they have foreseen such a diabolical instrument in the hands of children with little or no religious upbringing, I am sure the First and Second Amendments would have been differently written.

During World War II, our army officers were issued .45-caliber Colt automatic pistols. I carried one for eighteen months in Europe. I carried it from the time I waded ashore at Utah Beach until our forces linked up with the Russians in Czechoslovakia. During this whole period, I saw a pistol fired only one time; that one time, a pistol went off while it was being cleaned. (It narrowly missed me.) I never heard of any officer firing this weapon in anger. It did not take me long to figure out that a carbine was more effective in a fire fight. I got one early and it was the weapon that gave me a measure of security.

The world is ever changing. Laws, too, are written that suit the period of time in which the writers lived. Our First and Second Amendments were right and proper in their day, but they need changes today. I treat concerns about the First Amendment in later chapters.

In 1939 the Supreme Court ruled that a sawed-off shotgun was not a military weapon and did not qualify for protection under the Second Amendment. The ruling was a result of a federal law that required registration of sawed-off shotguns. The National Rifle Association and their followers claim constitutional rights for pistols. Considering the 1939 Supreme Court decision, I cannot see how the pistol advocates can logically make such a claim. I feel sure that if the matter were to arrive at the Supreme Court today, it would suffer the same fate as the sawed-off shotgun.

This country has, in various states, some unhappy people who have banded themselves into groups, and call themselves "citizen militias." They pride themselves by labeling themselves "patriots." I believe they are truly patriots, and they wish to be ready in case our country is in danger. What I wish to forcefully bring to the attention of the gun lobby, however, is that these people are drilling with rifles (constitutionally speaking, muskets) not pistols. These people know well that at twenty-five yards or more, pistols are of little value when fighting an enemy. For gun lobby people to advocate pistols for the purpose of our national defense shows their absurdity or stupidity.

Much has been said and written about the fact that while there are many gun laws in this country, the person who would use a gun for improper purposes has no problem getting a gun—usually a handgun. Of course, this must be true. If one city or state has a gun law and an adjacent city or state has no such law, how could anyone expect that law in Area A to be effective in Area B? Area A cannot stop and examine every person going from B to A. If a burglar in Area B wants to use a gun in Area A, it is no problem for him.

Now if we had a federal law regarding handguns, and in order to have a pistol you needed to have a permit, and this law were enforced, then over a period of time the vast majority of handguns would diminish. Along with such a law an offer to buy up pistols for destruction, strict enforcement of a controlled sales policy, and a fine for having an unregistered pistol would soon take guns out of the hands of improper people.

Such a pistol law would, of course, cause a great howl from the gun lobby. They would say they have lost their constitutional right of national defense. I again repeat, for such defense, the Framers of our Constitution adopted the Second Amendment. Gun owners could still have their rifles. (That is still the best weapon for defense when needed by a militia; the purpose designated by the Second Amendment.)

To return to my subject of ethics (or the lack of them) in education: Many educators in our country advocate the return of religious teaching in our schools. I experienced just such a religious grounding in my early years at school and at Texas A & M University (then College) from 1928 to 1932. Every Sunday morning the entire cadet corps dressed in No. 1 uniform and marched to Guion Hall for a sermon. Various speakers would expound morals and virtues. These were not the kind that would expound any specific form of religion. But the benefits of living a clean, ethical life were well covered. I believe people who have known A & M graduates of those days would agree that such training has accomplished the results intended. While religion was not discussed, the great, universally recognized values that have emanated from religion were expounded. Such messages were strong, clear, and well accepted by the A & M students.

According to *The Wall Street Journal,* May 12, 1994, edition: "About a million children today attend an estimated 10,000 evangelical Protestant schools. The vast majority of these schools sprang up in the last 20 years, in the first widespread secession from the public school system since the emergence of Roman Catholic schools a century ago.

"The enrollment of Catholic schools declined in recent years. The enrollment is once again climbing at the rate of about 10% each year. Many other private schools are growing."

Our schools today are on the defensive, as many parents of children in school are not satisfied with the education received by their children. Of course, when you check the quality of our schoolchildren's performance against that of other industrial nations, the inferiority is quite discernible. When the scholastic ability of children today is compared with earlier years by grade level, again we are disappointed. It is quite clear what is wrong. The various reports sketched out in chapter 2 answer this: Lack of enforced home motivation, unchecked disturbances by students at school, and lack of desire to learn sum it up.

As a result, many parents who have the know-how are now teaching their children at home. Much objection is made by school authorities, but courts have been approving home-schooling.

Other parents, who wish to send their children to private schools, are pressuring their states to permit school money to go to defray tuition for their children wherever the parents see fit. Parents find their children improve scholastically and are out of danger at parochial schools. However, if such a funding trend ever develops, it will certainly hurt our public school system as we know it.

Other industrial nations teach their students certain technical skills and a work ethic that together prepare the high school graduate to fit in quickly to work in the business world. I believe such training and such an ethical grounding would be welcomed by our students and create greater interest in their studies. It would also save industry time and money when putting new people to work.

A grounding in basic ethical mores is essential. We must teach children these, not only the courses we now prescribe in our schools. We cannot wait and hope that scientists will identify and "program" a gene that will cause newborns to carry over the wisdom and knowledge of their parents. It will never happen.

For several years I have been questioning my twelve grandchildren about their schooling—because I have not been happy with the results I believe should be evident at various grade levels. An October 11, 1993 *Wall Street Journal* article, "Kids' Homework May Be Going the Way of the Dinosaur" pretty well answered my questions by its very title. Author Gabriella Stern writes, in part:

"In both public and private schools, many teachers are assigning less homework, and fewer students are completing the assignments. Parents do not seem to care as much as they used to. When Yankelovich Partners and the cable network Nickelodeon polled 1,200 children earlier this year, 83% of teenagers aged 14 to 17 said it's important to their parents that they complete their homework, down from 96% in 1987.

"Educators blame the changing American household. They cite work-weary parents who lack the energy to nag their children, as well as fractured families in which no one watches the young ones. Some parents place too much emphasis on their children's extracurricular activities—sports teams, music lessons and the like. By the time their children get home from soccer practice and karate, they're too tired to buckle down to academics."*

And what about higher education? Anyone interested in the state of education in our universities may wish to read a new book written by George Roche, President of Hillsdale College. That book is *The Fall of the Ivory Tower: Government Funding, Corruption, and the Bankrupting of American Higher Education. Insight* magazine published a special cover story report naming this as "Book of the Year." Excerpts and favorable reviews have appeared in dozens of sources, from *Reader's Digest* to *The Wall Street Journal*. The main theme of this convincing book is the role played by the federal government in degrading and destroying American higher education.

The thrust of Roche's book was to some extent summarized in a message Jack Kemp recently delivered at Hillsdale College titled "A Cultural Renaissance." In part, that message reads as follows:

"A government conceived in liberty has none of the tools of tyranny. It cannot enforce the savage 'virtue' of the French Revolution, or shape the socialist 'New Man.' It depends instead, on other institutions—structures between the individual and the state—that instill character, purpose, and virtue. Churches and synagogues that

---

* Reprinted from *The Wall Street Journal,* October 11, 1993.

raise a moral standard. Parents who provide a moral and spiritual example to their children. Schools that teach not only the basics of math and history, but the basics of citizenship and character—lessons that come from an understanding of the Decalogue as well as the Declaration of Independence."

As we examine what is going on in Russia today, we can well see the results of the seventy-year absence of the teachings about which Jack Kemp speaks. The society in Russia, and particularly their business leaders, seem to be lacking completely in ethics. In the absence of morals, the rule of the jungle is rampant.

CHAPTER 4

A Look Back: Before the Breakdown

Over 200 years ago, the Framers of our Constitution could not look into a crystal ball and see the extent to which the effective shedding of religion in so many homes would affect the well-being of our citizens. In those long-ago days, nonbelievers and nonpracticing religious families were neither common nor envisioned as becoming the near-norm. Every child was brought up in a religious environment, at home and at school. Our earliest schools of higher learning were religious in origin and (to some extent) emphasis. Children were brought up to adhere to moral norms and to obey the laws of the land. Madison, Hamilton, Jay, and their contemporaries could not foresee what would happen from their era till now, though they were filled with foreboding at what *might* develop were the religious element to fade or disappear from the lives of men. "Of all the dispositions and habits which lead to political prosperity," said President George Washington as he left office, "Religion and Morality are indispensable supports. . . . And let us with caution indulge the supposition that morality can be maintained without religion . . . reason and experience both forbid us to expect that national morality can prevail in exclusion of religious principle."

More recently, Jack Kemp was on target when he said, "People obey the law for one of two reasons. They either love God or fear punishment. When these break down, the result is an environment that breeds violence, poverty, and anarchy." Undeniably, the breakdown of those two factors is bearing fruit in our land today.

To stop the erosion of proper behavior among our youth and return them to a civil mindset, two things must be done. First, if we cannot teach religion in our schools, we should at least teach and affirm the norms that five thousand years of Judeo-Christian religion have shown acceptable to all people and have served as a reliable guide for civilized behavior. Second, we should teach sound core subjects while affirming such basic norms as integrity, fair play, and observance of law.

The Bible that Jews and Christians revere contains the story of a woman named Hannah, who wished for a son to be born to her. She went to the House of the Lord and was told by Eli the Priest to "go in peace, and the God of Israel will grant thy petition." In time Hannah bore a son and named him Samuel. As soon as he was weaned, he was brought to the House of the Lord and turned over to Eli with instructions that he be lent to the Lord as long as he lived. According to Scripture, Samuel grew and ministered unto the Lord with Eli the priest.

The sons of Eli were evil men who dealt contemptuously in their service to the Lord. In one of Israel's many wars with the Philistines, Eli's sons were killed, Israel lost the war, and Eli died as a result. Samuel who then became the judge, or leader, of Israel, exhorted the Israelites to be righteous, and defeated the Philistines.

Here is a story that illustrates an irrefutable axiom: A child reared with a purpose and guided correctly, even amid a bad environment, will most often grow up straight and true.

Since time out of mind, wise parents have heeded the maxim, "Train a child in the way he should go, and when he grows up he will never depart from it." Unfortunately, too many parents today do not know this old and proven proverb, or do not care to practice such training. Children who grow up neglected and are allowed to find their own interests will likely join the ranks of our problem children.

To expand upon this and examine what has happened to our contemporary young people, I wish to look back over my eighty-plus years to contrast the youth of today with those of an earlier period in this century.

I was born in Russia to Jewish parents, and came to this country at three-and-a-half years of age. After arriving at the port of Galveston, we moved on to Dallas County. There I was reared on a dairy farm on the south side of the Trinity River. (That dairy, Schepps Dairy, is now the largest in Texas.) When I started school in the 1920s, I knew no English, but that was no impediment. The school I attended, Bonnie View, had four rooms. The principal was a Baptist minister. There were two—and, later, three—teachers, who together taught nine grades.

Every morning began with a fifteen-minute assembly, a time devoted to prayer, the singing of religious songs, and a short sermon by the principal. My parents learned of this religious service but were not disturbed. They knew my upbringing in faith at home could not be supplanted. Reminders of good morals were constant in my parents' home; my mother frequently admonished, "In your conduct with people, always be a man." Her message was clear; it meant: in all engagements with others, deal honestly and ethically.

(As I look back at those early years, I cannot help but dwell on the current advocacy for religion in school by many today. I must add that I have no doubt that religion would be of help, though how much help is uncertain. For evaluation, consider the large number of parochial schools in existence today. You will find those schools do not have the overwhelming problems of our public schools. While the Constitution forbids the establishment of a state religion, nowhere have I seen a prohibition upon teaching the morals deemed acceptable by our great religions. It would be of great value if those morals were taught, or at least affirmed, to children in our classrooms today. While this seems unlikely at present, I will propose a reasonable substitute in the next chapter.)

At school, main topics of study were reading, writing, and arithmetic. The subjects other than these contributed to proper living, civil behavior, and character building. I believe such subjects are just as important today, if not more so, than they were in those days. I name them below and offer a few reasons for their importance, though there are more.

Geography was one such subject, taught at several grade levels. The texts were liberally adorned with pictures of the people of many lands. These pictures showed the people at work, their native dress, what they ate, various crops, animals, climate, rivers, mountains, and many other facts. All of these together were discussed in class. Students were encouraged to compare themselves and their customs with people of other nations.

Civics, also, was taught at several levels. Besides being taught to be good citizens, we were introduced to the fundamentals of civil and criminal law. Before leaving Bonnie View, every student participated in a trip to the

Dallas County Courthouse. Here an official of the court lectured us on why we have courts, explaining to us how much better it is to argue out a problem or misunderstanding to reach judicial resolution than to fight and kill. After we left the court, where a trial was always in progress, we were taken to the county jail. A look at the steel bars and doors was enough to shake up each of us. The real shocker, though, was when we were taken into the gallows chamber.

We were taught history in every grade. U.S. and Texas history books were full of pictures of the men and women who figured prominently in our nation's history. Every important person in our history books was studied, along with the role he or she played in the building of our state and country. Research at the library was frequently required of us, and written compositions were turned in regularly.

During those years at Bonnie View, we had hygiene classes in at least two grades. Here again the books were filled with pictures. I can still remember a picture of a boy smoking and another of the same boy with no cigarette in his mouth and no smoke swirling about his face. The contrast was starkly convincing. Also, I remember other pictures contrasting a boy who had combed his hair and wore neat-looking clothes with the same boy who did not so care about his appearance. The author of that textbook certainly knew how to assemble helpful, memorable material on the subject of health.

I mention the above for a very definite reason: I believe the chief focus during formative years, at school and at home, should be in learning to be an upright, clean-living person of good morals and character who demonstrates respect for other persons.

In discussing this matter, we inevitably must face the issue of corporal punishment. The young man Michael Fay, who got in trouble in Singapore, has brought the subject of spanking children to the forefront within the last two years. It was quite startling to American liberals, the ACLU, and their followers to find that so many other Americans agreed with Fay's punishment. Certainly, caning is too harsh. But for centuries the adage "Spare the rod and spoil the child" was the rule, and since paddling has generally been brought to a stop, it is plain to see what has happened. At Bonnie View, children were paddled by the principal for several infractions. One of them was fighting. (I was paddled once for fighting—the only time I was ever punished at school.) All the children at Bonnie View feared a paddling more than any other punishment. Some who received such punishment at school received the same at home afterward. The stigma for such punishment and the inevitable ribbing received from the schoolmates made paddling very much something to be avoided. I do not remember, from my boyhood, any parent complaining to the teacher of the school system about being unfair in punishment. But teachers today not only fear their pupils, they also worry about what action parents and the school administration will take—against them. A suggestion: give approval to teachers and school principals to paddle children who come to school to make trouble for teachers, and this will put a swift end to many of these problems. Indeed, the old adage, "Spare the rod and spoil the child," would, if resurrected, clear up quickly many problems teachers have in class today.

Our dairy farm was, of course, in a rural area. Within three-quarters of a mile from us was a black community.

Also nearby were farms owned by whites. Our milk-processing plant, home, barns, and chicken house were always unlocked. Still, we never had a theft.

In those days, all able-bodied men had jobs. Very few women had jobs outside the home, having plenty to do on the domestic front. Sewing, cooking, cleaning, washing clothes, and raising children was a full-time job. On the farm, children had more to do than did their counterparts in the city; every child had chores to complete, when not in school. Play was limited to marbles, tops, hoop-rolling, baseball, foot races, pole-vaulting, and other such sports. All children did lots of reading. For spending money, I (like many of my friends) trapped rabbits, picked cotton at a neighbor's farm, plucked mistletoe from trees, picked pecans, and raised pigeons. Our lives were not all work, though. Occasionally, I went to see the Dallas Steers play baseball. If I did not have fifteen cents to get in, I asked if my cousin Julius Schepps (part-owner of the Steers) was there. If he was, he would let me in free. If not, I went home. (During and after the regular season, the players held jobs other than playing ball, for the baseball salaries of the 1990's were far distant.)

On every farm there were firearms. Every boy knew how to aim and fire a rifle or shotgun. We all quickly learned how dangerous these were and knew how to handle them safely. No one was ever injured with guns, at least around where I lived. In those days, I never heard of a juvenile using a weapon—not a gun, not even a stick—in anger. We did have fights, occasionally, but it was always with fists. We had our differences, but never did anybody seek to permanently injure someone, much less kill someone.

In those days, young people knew one another for an extended period of time before getting married. They married only after they were reasonably sure of their future together. Living together before marriage was absolutely unknown. Divorces were few. Divorced persons were frowned upon. Children being born to unwed mothers was a rarity that most certainly took place in secrecy. Such children were stigmatized by the descriptive word "bastard."

People worked hard, long hours to get by. A week's wages for a sixty-hour week of menial work was close to fifteen dollars. This would support a small family, though the wives had to make the family's clothes and be very thrifty when purchasing food. Times being what they were, thrift was essential. A pound of sugar was five cents; a pound of coffee was nineteen cents; and for those who had a car, gasoline was fifteen to nineteen cents per gallon. In those days the expression "sound as a dollar" was applied to the best of a product or to a good man. At that time, when Ford Motor Company announced a wage hike to thirty-five dollars per week, it was top news. One of my sisters married a successful shoe salesman who was paid thirty-five dollars a week for his efforts; he was considered a good wage earner.

Everybody worked. There was no unemployment compensation, though people helped one another when someone unfortunate needed help. A person who got hurt on the job anywhere had little more than relatives and friends to fall back on. Unlike today, there were no unanswered job advertisements. There was no wave of Mexican, Central American, and Caribbean people crossing our borders for open jobs, for nearly every job had a taker.

During the period from 1917 to 1930 in our area, there were no phones and no electric lights. In the evening, we studied by the light of kerosene lamps. Only very few people had yet bought automobiles. Of course, television, computers, and many other of today's luxuries had not been invented. The average amount of a family's personal possessions was very meager. In spite of such circumstances, I believe the average person at that time was much more content than are those today who have much. Certainly few children of that day were out trying to steal and commit other serious crimes.

Businesses were closed every Sunday, so people got to stay home at least one day a week. Families could get together for socials and for a good Sunday lunch or dinner. Of great importance was the fact that closing business gave people a chance for solace and prayer at church. And children went to church as well. I believe that today, if we could return to that practice, it would help much toward solving many of our family problems. The vast number of businesses that open on Sunday not only deny their workers a day off that they should spend with their families, but also lure shoppers away from a needed weekly experience.

Looking at the difference between children growing up in the 1920s and today, I can understand the problems confronting children today. To start with, a great number of them are being brought into this world by parents who have no grounding in the fundamentals of religion. We have children born to men and women who stay together only a short while. Children are born to single mothers who can barely earn a living for themselves. There are children born to parents who work at poor-paying jobs. In general, such parents themselves received very little education and have little or no time for their children. Many children are left shattered after their parents go through a difficult divorce. There are children in well-to-do families who are given too many material things and whose lives are left void of proper guidance. If you examine the many children who go wrong, you will find many other reasons for the problems children encounter today. Add to the lives of these unattended children a mixture of sleazy television programs and the general run of our motion pictures today, dope, tobacco, guns, gangs, rap music, the job of owning the newest of new cars (even if stolen), and so on, and it is easy to understand how we have gotten where we are.

In *The Wall Street Journal* of April 12, 1994, there is a scientific explanation of this phenomenon. It says the following:

"Out-for-life may be the punishment for many of America's children who get little or no attention, nurturing or intellectual stimulation in the first three years of their lives." Scientists tell us that much of a child's brain development occurs during the first three years of life, and that environmental influences, both favorable and unfavorable, have a lot to do with how children are shaped for life.

According to this report, researchers believe that nature acts like a sculptor throughout childhood, chiseling away at brain cells that are not used and nurturing those that are. In other words, if a baby spends his first months of life lying unattended in his crib and later watching witless television shows, the brain cells needed to learn math, literature, and the arts will have atrophied to a considerable extent by the time the child enters school. Even worse, negative influences such as stress and abuse can lead to mental retardation, learning disabilities, and emotional problems throughout the life of a child.

The *Journal* article followed the release of a report by a Carnegie Foundation panel comprised of a wide cross-section of experts from the world of economics and politics. The report contained the same disturbing message: Millions of young children are so deprived of proper care and intellectual stimulation that their growth into healthy and responsible adults is threatened.

The reason for this state of affairs, the panel concludes, is that too many of our parents are being overwhelmed by poverty, teenage pregnancy, divorce, or overwork.

Individuals within society have suggested many ways to slow down this rapid devolution, but there has been no real attempt at implementing a workable plan, much less evidence of any behavioral turnaround. I believe the only solution is an all-encompassing program that will begin early in the schooling of our children and properly engage their thought processes as they grow up.

CHAPTER 5

Further Thoughts on the Decline of Religion in America

On December 10, 1993, President Clinton said, "The vacuum of values is the root of violence." He declared that the nation must fight violence with values, saying "Guns, drugs, and violence fill the vacuum where the value of civilized life used to be." In our country, the now-declining civilized life to which Mr. Clinton referred came into being because of our ancestors' adherence to Judeo-Christian norms and beliefs.

Jeanne Kirkpatrick expresses best the source of the great morals and values that guided our country in the following statement: "There is, I think, only one revolutionary society in the contemporary world, and that is our society. It is so revolutionary that it's not clear that any of us can finally bear the daring thrust to the realization of the age-old values that our American revolution contains and celebrates.

"Those values are the definitive values of the Judeo-Christian civilization. They have inspired every authentically Judeo-Christian society in history. Those values declare, above all, the irreducible worth and uniqueness of every individual."

Children brought up in dysfunctional families and in homes devoid of proven civilizing values are the primary problem-makers today. If we reflect for a moment on where our proven values and morals came from, I believe we can readily agree that they came from Judeo-Christian teaching. The early settlers of this country and the Framers of our Constitution were guided by these teachings. If we look into the homes where troubled children come from, we will find little or no religious teaching passed along or observed there. Some vague semblance of right and wrong may be known to such children, but there is no deep-seated effort made to instill virtue in such children. Also, the observance of law means little to those, depending to a great extent, as these children do, upon their perceptions of the mere likelihood of getting caught.

In *The Houston Chronicle* of July 2, 1994, religion editor Cecile Homes White wrote, "As America celebrates its 218th birthday, religious leaders, talk show hosts, political candidates and special interest groups are waging a star-spangled battle for the public's allegiance.

"The civic morality Americans once took for granted has eroded, resulting in widespread disagreement over which values are American values.

"The rhetoric obscures a quieter, more serious discussion of what lies behind the nation's growing urban blight, its citizenry's distrust of once-respected institutions and its young people's cynicism. The debate is taking place as the nation enjoys an unusual spiritual renewal with people searching for life's deeper meaning in religions as diverse as paganism and fundamentalism.

"Complicating this complex discussion is the nation's growing religious and ethnic pluralism. Once Protestant Christianity took center stage in America, obscuring other voices, including Roman Catholics' and Jews'. Now, public life also is influenced by Buddhists, Muslims, and

Hindus. In a nation founded upon the concept of religious freedom, religion has become something of a sore subject. . . .

"Lost is the deeper question of how the nation might regain a common understanding of civic virtue, professional ethics and personal morality in the final decade of the 20th century.

"In simple language, how do you teach little children to love their neighbors as themselves and then grow into adults who live accordingly?

"In schools, offices and sanctuaries, Americans are searching for answers."*

In his final words to the nation, former President Richard Nixon said, "From the 1960s on, our laws and our mores have been driven by the cultural conceits that took hold during the heyday of the counterculture, including a denial of personal responsibility and the fantasy that the coercive power of government can produce spiritual uplift, cure poverty and bigotry, legislate growth, and stamp out any number of individual and social inadequacies.

"The founders created a land of opportunity. For more than three centuries, opportunity was enough because the culture conditioned people to take advantage of it. But we have created a culture in which appallingly large numbers ignore the opportunities offered by work, choosing instead those offered by the interwoven worlds of welfare and crime. Our task now is not to invent but to enforce honest work as the route to it. We need to get America back on track before it sails off into the abyss."

Mr. Nixon could have added that the land of opportunity our founders created was deeply influenced by Judeo-Christian teachings.

I do not believe anyone would suggest that we legislate religion in the home. Surely we cannot force parents to teach their children morals. So how can children who have had no such teaching be brought up to embrace the norms of civilization? For these norms must be inculcated while children's minds are malleable.

Children have plenty of capacity to learn and understand. It is a matter of *what* they are exposed to and *which* values are emphasized. Will it be what they see on TV, in the movies, on the street, in the lyrics of rap music, the advice of gang leaders—or what civilization has long considered the better way? The problem, at present, is that they see too much of the trendy but destructive ways of the wrong people. If we lead our children correctly through their early years and into their teenage period when their ability to reason begins to mature, we will have far less reason to fear that they will go astray. The absolutely essential starting point is to prevent children from getting off on the wrong foot, for once they have started wrong, it is difficult to straighten them out.

How can we get children started on the right path? There is a way, and if that objective cannot be accomplished in the home, then society is compelled to step in with a solution. Within society, the most logical place for the inculcation of civil belief and conduct is the school.

What should be the scholastic guide for a curriculum for ethics? Further, how do we actively affirm morality grounded in religion without violating the Constitution and alienating those who oppose any evidence of religion in our schools?

I believe the best answer would result if the leaders of our great religions in America would get together regarding this problem and map out a course of teaching that would cover the ethics they hold in common—and which are unknown to many of our children. This course of study could embody much, if not all, of the teaching that has civilized mankind, without teaching religion itself. Surely, every religion teaches many, if not all, of the norms and values that are lacking in too many of our children. Our religious leaders would surely agree that children, so taught, would most likely later seek a personal religious faith on their own, while adhering to the basics in the meantime.

If the above cannot be accomplished, or is too long in coming about, then school districts should assemble their own curricula for teaching right and wrong. The Constitution and laws of the U.S., including the laws of every state and city, cover the most serious deviations in conduct among our youth. To augment this, specially trained teachers should be brought into our school systems to cover this tremendously important subject.

A great majority of our citizens agree that absence of a religious element in the lives of our children is an important factor leading to delinquency. Much good would be accomplished if our president would summon our nation's religious leaders to Washington for a great convocation and charge them with coming up with a course of study in ethics acceptable to our people, to be taught in our public schools. Such teaching would go far in curbing the great increase in juvenile delinquency nationwide. This is not to say that religion is the sole answer to the problems of our youth. I do, however, emphasize that the lessons offered by religion play a most important part in shaping the behavior of our experience, study, and practice. To ignore these lessons would be foolish.

In centuries past, people in every land knew that for children to grow up to be virtuous they must be molded from day one. The number one problem in the raising of children today is that too many of them just grow up. Period. There is no adequate spiritual mooring for so many of them. Fortunately, the majority of our children are reared in homes where parents are financially able to properly provide for their children's welfare, are devoted to their children and safeguard them from harm, see that they value their school and studies, and make sure they are shielded from such disturbing elements as guns, dope, alcohol, tobacco, and so on. Those children who are not so fortunate are at risk, having no alternative influence to hold them in line.

If getting ever tougher on juvenile crime were the answer to the increasing problems of our country, we would have solved those problems by now. The truth is that people bent on crime think little (if at all) about the consequences of their acts, especially when the threat of punishment is uncertain. Such people are motivated to act illegally only by their desires at the time of their actions.

The best and only deterrent is to instill proper moral direction in children from the day of their earliest schooling. Such teaching of morals must be delivered to all children. I believe the vast majority of children can be taught right from wrong. If we do not expend the effort to do so, however, these children will be caught up in the world of violence, promiscuity, and robbery that they observe. Without a strong brake on their passions, children are overcome by them. For the purpose of instilling moral direction, a new and separate department should be adopted in our school systems. As I mentioned a bit earlier, teachers who have been specially trained to teach and observe the problems of children should be made a new, regular element in our schools to teach what I term Civilized and Acceptable Behavior (CAB).

The responsibility and curriculum of CAB teachers is outlined in the next chapter.

CHAPTER 6

Take a CAB: Teach Civilized And Acceptable Behavior

In an address delivered at Hillsdale College's Shavano Institute for National Leadership in 1994, Jack Kemp asked, "How do we respond when graves are filled by boys not old enough to shave? When girls not yet in their teens are taught how to use condoms, but not the responsibilities of motherhood? When poverty grows rampant among the ruins of families? When despair paralyzes responsibility and initiative? And when unemployment leaves 50 to 60 percent of males on the streets of some urban ghettoes and barrios?"

The former congressman and Secretary of Housing and Urban Development went on to say that "we can conclude that America's most urgent question is this enduring question: How do we instill the values of our parents in the lives of our children? The National Commission on Children concluded its 1993 report with the somber words: Today, too many young people seem adrift, without a steady moral compass to direct their daily behavior or to plot a responsible course for their lives.

"While this remains true, there will never be enough police and prisons to end the lawlessness in our streets if it starts in our hearts. There will never be enough government policies and welfare programs to conquer the

poverty of the spirit. And there will never be enough prosperity to bring the peace for which we long. To me, this is
the real meaning of the 'culture war.' It is not conducted
between battling spokesmen from the left and right. It is
not won or lost at the end of an election. It is a battle for
the souls of our children, for the strength of our families
for the peace of our neighborhood. Its victories are won
in individual lives, but its outcome depends on the
strength of cultural standards."

As if in answer to Kemp's question, former President
Bush delivered an address to graduates of the John Coo-
per School in Houston on May 4, 1994 in which he said,
"There is a moral emptiness among American youth and
society as a whole that can be solved if educators and the
U.S. school system would teach family values.

"How can schools remain neutral on this most essential battlefield?" Indeed, why have schools gone out of
their way not to teach values? Values include, Bush emphasized, tolerance, decency, fairness, courage, honesty,
self-discipline, and respect. "The symptoms of America's
moral emptiness are problems with violent crime, crack
cocaine and teen sex."

Jack Kemp summarized and asked the right question. And George Bush has given the correct answer. His
answer is in line with what I concluded several years ago,
before I began writing this book to document that answer.

Many programs are being instituted throughout our
country to try to control the deterioration in conduct of
children in our schools. While some improvement may
occur here and there, the major turnaround for which we
have waited is not in sight. We can continue to pass ever-
harsher penalties for criminal behavior, we can spend
more money for prisons and defense; all miss the target.
Children who are not properly taught at an early age and

are exposed to the detrimental influences that seek their attention, are incapable of understanding the penalties that will result from deviation. We can achieve such a goal if we set out with an all-inclusive system, which will include many of the programs that have been tried or are in force by many communities and/or school districts. The system I advocate would become part of a child's schooling from the first day he or she enters school at the earliest level, and will remain in place until a high school diploma is achieved.

I do not propose that we indoctrinate our youth with thoughts and ideas contrary to the principles of freedom that we as Americans hold dear. What has been fought for and found good should remain. But if we continue following the status quo, those underlying principles of liberty under law could be destroyed. We could one day find ourselves facing an autocratic government, one that would enforce law and order in a despotic rather than democratic style.

How can we obtain the objective we all want? The first step would be to establish in each school a program that would teach every child Civilized and Acceptable Behavior (CAB). Teachers for this course of study would be specialized and be solely responsible for the proper molding of our children in civilized and acceptable behavior. As part of their responsibilities, these CAB teachers would be attuned to identifying troubled children and securing for them proper help as benefits each case. A child may be in need of food, clothing, or shelter. A child may be getting molested, mistreated, or neglected. In any case, CAB teachers must have an answer, and no child should be forced to continue in any unfortunate circumstance. To so neglect a child will surely result in delinquency in the future. We must consider this fact: that at least one-half of our prison inmates were so neglected.

Important elements of a curriculum of study offered by the CAB instruction include:

1. The importance of learning, and of securing a high school diploma.
2. The importance of attaining and maintaining good health.
3. The importance of respect for others, regardless of racial and ethnic differences.
4. The virtue of helpfulness.
5. The essential importance of good morals.
6. The importance of knowing how to handle disagreements without resorting to violence.
7. The wisdom of joining only acceptable organizations, not gangs.
8. The importance of discipline, learning to mind one's parents, guardians, and teachers.
9. The wisdom of avoiding and running from weapons.
10. The importance of obeying laws.
11. The importance of staying away from alcohol, drugs, and tobacco.
12. The importance of taking personal responsibility for one's decisions and actions.
13. The wisdom of refraining from premarital and extramarital sex, with men and boys learning respect for women.
14. The dignity of work and satisfaction derived by earning one's way, rather than asking for charity.

The CAB teacher should observe all students that he/she may be responsible for. CAB teachers should also network and converse with all the other teachers in school, in an effort to quickly discover any troubled students and take quick corrective action. Properly conducted, such a program will cause students themselves to do the legwork and identify violators of the rules. Troubled children should be questioned, and if help for such children is needed, the Children's Protective Agency should be called in.

There are many problems that can befall children that our schools are not looking for and thus go unattended. CAB teachers, whose job it would be to look for such unfortunates, could discover and help such children. Below are a few examples, culled from *Time* magazine:

"A juvenile judge tells of a 10-year-old—a precocious lad straight from a Dickens novel—who has been through court now for his fifth felony. The child breaks into houses.

"The judge finally takes him out of his home environment and sends him to a local children's home, where they discover that he may have been breaking into other people's homes because he was hungry. . . .

"A teacher in an inner-city school tells about an activity she devised to make learning fun for her students. As part of an exercise, she popped popcorn. She noticed that one little boy was holding on to his bag of popcorn dearly. She asked him, 'Don't you like popcorn?' He replied, 'Oh yes, ma'am, I do. But I'm going to take this home to my little brother. He hasn't had anything to eat today.' . . .

"A former teacher in a poor school district tells of two young brothers who did very well in school when they were there. Problem was, they were absent a lot. When she looked into it, she saw a pattern: They were never absent at the same time. When she asked why, she got the answer: They had only one pair of shoes, and they took turns wearing them to school."

The November 21, 1994 edition of *Time* magazine carries an article by Jon D. Hull regarding runaway children. This article tells of the sordid predicaments that befall 1.3 million of our children each year. All of these children leave home because of the lack of real home and poor parental care. A CAB program in a school could quickly identify these children and save them from the hell they meet on the streets.

The instruction given children should, of course, be changed as these children progress from one grade level to another. The instruction should always accent the importance of a high school education as well as Civilized and Acceptable Behavior. No child should be permitted to forget these two goals. Our jails and prisons are loaded with former children who did not obtain either.

We hear much about peer pressure among our adolescent youth. This phenomenon consists of nothing more than a few "machos" who step out boldly and lead others to do things that right-thinking children would not do. If we teach our children the art of proper CAB, we can turn that around. The peer pressure could come from the children who are prone to proper conduct. As part of their training, children should be taught that they are their brothers's keeper. When they see their peers going wrong, they should use their superior peer pressure to bring such children in line. If all children are taught the correct way of living, then when one of them steps out of line, they will reason with and bring the violator into line. Some parents may object and declare that their child does not need that type of instruction. In truth, such parents must be led to understand that if their child understands the problems, they can well prevent other children from falling prey. Properly taught and inspired children can do more to police those of their peers than can an army of police officers. We need only to show them the way.

Children now start school at age five. By that time they have already seen and heard too much violence on TV. Many have already experienced it in their homes or on the streets of their neighborhood. Children are influenced by and grow to believe that what they see and hear is correct and acceptable. During those early years, their inquisitive and keen minds seek and record every incident that they experience. During this period of their lives, they formulate a perspective on what they perceive to be right or wrong. During those years, society must compete for what those minds perceive to be correct. If we exercise the efforts that are required and are at our disposal, we can win over their thought processes. Our sages of centuries past learned that a child properly guided from infancy would walk upright on the straight path when grown. Our traditional two-parent, religious home did this well through 1950s. This is no longer the case in too many homes. Society must add an extra dimension to make up for this most important missing ingredient.

Herewith is an explanation of the elements of the proposed CAB curriculum:

1. *Importance of learning.* Many of our students go to school feeling that their parents send them there just to get them out of the house. And when teachers require them to abide by rules and study, the students' suspicions are confirmed. Parents of these children never explain how important an education is. Some parents actually do not care if their children get an education or not. Many children have no parental guidance at all. A single-parent, working mother holding two jobs, a troubled family, an alcoholic family gives little or no guidance to children. The school must provide guidance in this regard.

2. *Good health rules should be taught.* A child should know such basics as brushing teeth, bathing, wearing clean clothes, etc. With the growing popular emphasis on proper nutrition, the fundamentals of this important matter should be a part of the curriculum. There is much that can be presented to children to lead them to eat more healthful meals. Our school lunchrooms should reflect what our children learn in class.

3. *Respect for others.* It is never too early to teach children to respect one another. We should also teach them to respect their elders. When I was in school, you said, "No, ma'am" or "Yes, ma'am" when talking to a teacher or elders. I felt I should show respect by so doing. I have had teachers tell me they do not wish such show of respect. Such teachers say a "no" or "yes" is sufficient. Once a child feels his or her familiarity with a teacher or parent does not require a show of respect, that child will lack the attitude that promotes the respect necessary for proper guidance.

4. *Helpfulness.* There are many facets of helpfulness. Those are virtues that children should acquire and respect for the good feeling that goes with it. It also should be shown how it will pay dividends. Many illustrations can be shown by the teacher. Helping a fellow student with homework or picking up a dropped book must occur often in a school. Helping a parent at home with any number of chores should become a desire on the part of a child. From what I hear, many parents say today their children need such training.

5. *Ethics.* Fortunately, the vast majority of children come from homes that are religiously oriented. These students are less likely to go off on a wrong path. However, they can fall into the wrong company and become statistics on crime reports. The big problem results from the many

unfortunate homes where morals and ethics training is deficient. Children from these homes have no mooring. They are apt to drift in whatever direction the tide flows. The teaching of basic ethics in schools would be of tremendous benefit for such children.

It would be of inestimable value if our great religions in America could agree on a curriculum of morals and ethics to be taught in our schools. Our school administrators should push our community religious leaders to come up with such a curriculum. There is no reason, however, that we cannot develop a curriculum that would embody federal laws, state laws, and laws of our communities. If all of these were taught well, our children would be morally well equipped. I see no reason why religious leaders could not be invited to classrooms so long as they stick to a set of guidelines. Nor do I see any reason why the tenets of religion cannot be taught without promoting a given religion.

6. *Disagreements and violence.* The violence seen by children on TV, in movie theaters and, unfortunately, on our streets should be a topic discussed often. Children should be most emphatically taught how wrong it is. They should fully understand how to solve a disagreement and avoid violence. They must understand that improper conduct and violence seen in movies and on TV is only for entertainment and for advertising products. The best solution they should be taught is to look for a program that teaches, or better yet, get books and read. Children of all ages should be given a list of books designed for their grade level. Such books should be easily obtainable. Better yet, the reading of books as part of homework should keep children so busy they will not watch the degrading TV programs that are so plentiful. Tests should be given

that will call forth evidence of the student's having read the prescribed books.

The suffering caused by violence should be discussed often. Local violence should be studied to the extent understood by the age of the student. Students should feel the suffering brought about because of violent incidents that occur in their community. Use of pictures of victims properly shown would have a profound effect. Police officers might be invited to talk to classes. I am sure police departments would be happy to cooperate.

7. *Joining organizations.* It is those aggressive, macho, undisciplined children who aspire to leadership and luxuries who organize gangs. Children who do not belong to a conventional two-parent home are likely to feel the gang is a good substitute for a family. Children should be taught to see through this falsehood. The drawbacks of belonging to the wrong group should be taught.

Examples of the wrongs perpetuated by gangs should be discussed. The students should be taught to report to their teachers anyone who participates in such activities. (The action to be taken by teachers after learning of such students is treated in the next chapter.)

8. *Discipline.* By and large most children in their earlier years mind their parents well. But problems begin to arise as early as ten years of age for some students. They often begin to think their parents are mean; generally this happens because the parents are merely trying to protect their children from some foolish notions. CAB teachers can be a big help in persuading such children that their parents and teachers know best, and that they should value parental guidance.

9. *Weapons.* Boys are naturally inquisitive. They see the great use of guns in the violent films they see in shows and on TV. Unfortunately, many see this in their streets.

When these boys get access to a gun, they experiment. Too often it leads to accidental shootings. I do not think we will see in the near future the removal of guns from the streets, and certainly not from homes. If parents would teach their children that guns kill, and show them what a bullet does when it strikes, children would respect firearms and not experiment with them. Of course, people who have ulterior motives are likely to secure a weapon in any way possible. For that reason, guns should be made difficult for children to obtain or find.

Police representatives of any city or community will gladly visit a classroom and discuss what weapons are made for and how dangerous they are. In fact, I believe it would be a real deterrent if children were taken to a firing range and permitted to fire a gun. Once a person has held a gun and seen what damage it can do, he will take care to use it properly, if at all.

Children cannot for long have a weapon in school or even in his possession off campus without some classmates knowing about it. CAB teachers who maintain good cordial relations with students will soon be informed of students who possess guns. Of course, the response to such information should be quick. Rewarding informers in regard to gun possession could be helpful; at the same time, students should know that such information, if brought to a teacher's attention, can save a life. They should not feel themselves to be "stool pigeons" if they tell.

10. *Obey laws*. There are always some young people who like to stand out, show off, and prove they are more macho than someone else by breaking the law. These people must be taught that lawbreaking does not pay, no matter what the crime. Particular attention should be paid to stealing, for children often pick up what they would like

to have, even if it belongs to another student. It is very important to curb this tendency at an early age. Many of our convicts started off with petty thievery. Thievery is probably the first improper behavior practiced by children, after lying. All other laws should be reviewed and enforced according to the age of the children in each CAB class.

11. *Alcohol, drugs, and tobacco.* Alcohol is available in many homes. A child who is not properly taught at home the proper usage of this substance is going to experiment and can quite likely become addicted at an early age. I believe that if CAB teachers make a good enough case academically by showing what detrimental effect alcohol can have on a person, such instruction will go far in preventing addiction. Certainly there is much documented evidence on this subject that can be covered.

Drugs of all kinds and their attendant dangers should be discussed often. The admonition "Just Say No" goes only so far in preventing drug use. This one problem, if brought to a halt (or even slowed appreciably) will save our country billions of dollars. And, of course, it would save lives and suffering. Police representatives would be happy to help in every way possible in the classroom. Much can be presented in class regarding the detrimental effect of drugs. Pictures of drug addicts suffering after years of usage would go far in discouraging a student from such experimentation. Former addicts are themselves available to talk to classes.

Instructional material detailing the dangers of smoking and the use of other tobacco products is plentiful. CAB teachers can find much material to help steer students away from experimenting with tobacco. I believe there are many doctors who would be glad to speak to children regarding the effect of tobacco.

12. *Personal responsibility.* CAB teachers should stress at every session that each person must make his own decisions and take responsibility for them. No one should allow a friend or alleged friend to push him or talk him into a situation counter to what makes for a good, healthy, educated, law-abiding citizen. A child who has been taught to stick to his beliefs and knows right from wrong will not easily be swayed by others to do wrong. Not only that, children should bring to the teacher's attention wrongdoers among them.

13. *Sex.* My Bible contains a sentence that reads, "Be fruitful and multiply." That admonition has been carried out faithfully by the human species. But in recent decades, man has perverted this directive. The act of sexual union itself has been practiced contrary to biblical teachings, to the point that pain and suffering have resulted and are increasing. Because of this we see children bearing children, the breaking up of homes, abuse and killing of unwanted children, abortion, and the spread of fatal and nonfatal diseases. The cost to society of children having children and of single-parent children is staggering. Such circumstances are the cause of much human suffering. The cost to society is great and ever increasing.

I do not feel qualified to tell such specialized teachers exactly what to say or do to help solve society's great problems with our youth and sex. But the six percent and greater incidence of teen pregnancies is alarming, and the greatest of efforts should be made to turn the corner on this crisis.

I also believe that society has been too tolerant and has not shown the disdain that should go with illegitimate births. Young people see it going on in Hollywood and thus consider it acceptable. Our government seems to approve this "lifestyle choice" by providing funds to mothers who are so disposed. More and better teaching of young girls and boys could greatly reduce this problem. Much is being done by a number of organizations to dissuade girls from losing their virginity. CAB teachers should solicit the help of these organizations, from which representatives should come to our schools and speak, even though there may be religious elements in their underlying beliefs.

Because of the sexual promiscuity today, some religious leaders believe that we as a people have sinned, and therefore HIV/AIDS has been visited upon society. Scientists generally disagree. Scientists, however, cannot disagree that if biblical patterns of proper sexual behavior were practiced by society, HIV/AIDS would disappear in one generation.

During their teen years, girls begin to want male companionship. During that period in life, they are highly vulnerable, for boys who like to brag of their sexual conquests are on the prowl. Just telling these girls to merely say no to these Romeos is not very helpful. Girls also see the romance on display in the movies and on TV, and they, as well as the boys who would rob them of their virginity, are infatuated. Male high school athletes are idols in girls' eyes; how can they resist? These girls must be taught that many boys are out for conquest.

There are the above aspects, and so much else that can be covered by CAB teachers to dissuade girls from giving up their virginity and risking the great possibility of pregnancy, disfavor, loss of education, permanent loss of the chance to earn a good income, loss of hope for a strong, successful marriage, disease, and even death.

Boys, too, should be taught these girls were not placed on this earth for their pleasure. They must understand that they must respect girls and women, not to molest and pressure them. Under the CAB system, any boy found to be pressuring girls for sex should be set straight in an appropriate manner. The method of teaching this subject and rules for enforcement should be left to the school or school system.

14. *Dignity of work.* Our government handouts have brought into being a considerable number of people who dodge work. They use every excuse possible to avoid working, preferring to line up for handouts from any one of the many governmental programs that have taught people how to get by without working. Our children's teaching must be instilled with the ethic that there is dignity in work.

All of the foregoing is indeed a departure from schools' objectives as we know them today. I am not a teacher and cannot evaluate the time that should be allocated for such subjects. But considering our current state, which is seemingly getting worse as time passes, change cannot be delayed. A system of education in clean living is absent in too many homes. Where else do we expect our children to obtain this necessary education? Our schools today furnish too many of our youth a platform from which to jump into gangs and vice. It must change!

Our youngsters are much more capable of understanding than we might generally expect. When you have a good message for children seven to eight and older to hear, you can see their eyes light up. They absorb lessons and remember well. But after a child has gone uninstructed ethically to the age of fifteen, he will tune you out. You have waited too late to teach him.

School districts generally are strapped for funds and may well object to the added cost of the CAB element.

Society, however, cannot afford to prevent the introduction of a remedy for our troubled youth. The millions and billions going into our police, judicial systems, jails, and prisons could be allocated elsewhere within ten years if we have the vision of what CAB schooling will do for our children, and institute such education.

CHAPTER 7
Surrogate Parent Homes

In spite of the promising results one would expect from CAB training in schools, we will have children who will turn out to be troublesome nonetheless. We will also find students who come from homes that are detrimental to their health and well-being in one or more ways. These are the children who are likely to become part of our future prison population. We cannot ignore these children. Provisions for them must be made available, for if we do not, they may well seek gang affiliation.

At present, such children don't finish school and, worse yet, wind up facing our police. At present, this prospect seems to be the future of such children who fall through the cracks. These children soon find how easy it is to "get off" each time they commit some offense, as society tries hard to rehabilitate offenders without inflicting permanent damage to them. These children soon get accustomed to arrests and releases as they become involved in more serious crimes. Detention facilities of various types are used to "recover" these children. Of course, some are reclaimed. But the rate of recidivism is too high for society to continue this process. After these children have taken the wrong road, the processes now used by society will not turn them around.

An alternative to the current methods of juvenile detention and methods of reclaiming these children is in place. It might be called a deep secret, since society is ignorant of this positive and great adventure in assuring the proper rearing of disadvantaged children and reclamation of those who have erred. I refer now to "parent homes." I don't know how many there are in existence, but I have visited three. These are in Hershey, Pennsylvania; Amarillo, Texas; and LaPorte, Texas. There are seven such homes I know of in Texas. There may be many more.

The homes I know of are governed by boards of directors composed of successful people from various backgrounds. The source of revenue consists of contributors who feel that these indeed are facilities that are of great benefit to society. As far as I know, none receive money or are in any way beholden to any governmental agency. They may receive government money for the upkeep of a child, but they refuse any attempt by government to mandate conditions.

Every parent home has at all times the maximum number of children it can care for. Of course, the limitation is the financial means of these homes. Some money comes from the families of the children being cared for, but not much. Every such home is deluged with requests that children, for various reasons, be accepted for parenting. Only a few of the requests are accepted.

I recently spent some time at Boys'/Girls' Harbor at LaPorte, Texas and Boys' Ranch at Amarillo, Texas. What follows is a brief description of the two.

LaPorte, Texas, is a small city about twenty-five miles east of Houston. Boys'/Girls' Harbor has been in existence there for about forty-seven years. Like Father Flanagan's Boys' Town in Omaha, Nebraska, it started out caring for orphaned children. This facility is supported by contributions from individuals, charitable organizations, and fund-raising affairs. It receives no public funds.

The children now at Boys'/Girls' Harbor come from dysfunctional or economically burdened families. Nearly 90 percent of the children are from single-parent homes. Children as young as five and up to high school age are taken in, and they can stay through their high school graduation. Upon entering, the children have little or no concept of a well-regulated home life. They know little or nothing about nutrition, eating etiquette, hygiene, dress, and courtesy. Few know what a toothbrush is. These children have been abused, but have not been in trouble with the law or acquired abusive habits. Although they are on the edge of becoming problematic to society, they can become good family members after a few months at Boys'/Girls' Harbor. Some have to be tutored for a while so that they can obtain a strong grasp of their schoolwork.

The housing at Boys'/Girls' Harbor consists of a number of cottages, eight at present. As more money is available and more unfortunate children can be accommodated, more cottages will be built. Six cottages are now occupied by boys and two by girls. As of April 1994, there were 68 boys and 16 girls at Boys'/Girls' Harbor. Each set of parents (man and wife) take care of eight children. Boys and girls are in separate cottages. Children are black, white, and brown. There is no discrimination by race or ethnicity. Every child goes to his or her church of choice every Sunday. Those who have no church background go to church with the house parents with whom they live.

Every child has chores, which depend on the age and ability of each child. Children wash dishes, make up beds, clean house, clean the campus, mow grass, gather pecans, and perform many other tasks.

Buses pick up the children for school at 7:30 A.M. and return the children at 4:00 P.M. When they return they have their assigned chores. At six o'clock they have dinner and then do their homework. There is no TV on school days. Pre-approved programs are permitted on Saturday and Sunday.

When not engaged in schoolwork or chores, the children have recreation of some form. Such games as softball, volleyball, and basketball are played. There is a recreation hall in which various other sports take place. A part-time sports director oversees these activities. The children are also involved in agricultural programs, such as 4-H and Future Farmers of America (FFA).

Ninety percent of those accepted at Boys'/Girls' Harbor are the children of single mothers who do not have the means to provide for their children. These mothers generally have been referred by someone in making the request that Boys'/Girls' Harbor care for their children. The mothers who overcome their difficulties and can again properly support their children reclaim them. Those that can't overcome their difficulties—generally drug addicts—are not that fortunate. The average child stays about two years before the mother overcomes her difficulties and reclaims her child. At the time I visited Boys'/Girls' Harbor, there was one child whose mother was in prison. Colin Rae, the director, told me of a mother who brought him four children not long ago. The children's ages were seven, eight, nine, and eleven. She had met with a financial setback, but within eight months, she had secured a good-paying job, had acquired a good home, and had reclaimed her children.

The LaPorte School District finds the children from Boys'/Girls' Harbor to be good students. They also find them to be as well behaved at school as they are at the home. They offer no disciplinary problems. One-half of these children are generally on the honor roll. Many who stay through high school graduation get scholarships and go on to college.

The home parents of these children are indeed dedicated people. Before joining Boys'/Girls' Harbor, they are thoroughly checked out. They range in age from late 20s to 50s.

The campus of Boys'/Girls' Harbor is clean and well kept in every regard. The cottages, the office building, and the several auxiliary buildings are brightly painted. The ladies working in the office are very friendly. No doubt all of this is indicative of the friendly, dedicated hard work of the director, Colin Rae.

During the visit to Boys'/Girls' Harbor, my wife, Manet, and I observed several of the house parents and a number of children. We were very impressed with the cordiality of these parents and noticed how contented the children were.

During the late summer of 1994, we visited Cal Farley's Boys' Ranch. This facility is located at an old ghost town of Tascosa, about sixty miles northwest of Amarillo. This parent home was started by Cal Farley, a man highly concerned about disadvantaged children. It was chartered as Cal Farley's Boys' Ranch in 1939 on 120 acres, along with the old courthouse. Cal Farley died in 1967. By 1994, this parent home had expanded to 10,000 acres and 60 buildings. The girls are housed in a separate facility called Girls' Town, an affiliate of Boys' Ranch.

Each parent home has a separate area for the parent and six bedrooms for the children. Each such bedroom accommodates three children. Necessary facilities go with each bedroom. Each home has sitting/recreation areas and may have a small kitchen were snacks may be prepared. The children study in their rooms. There is a central dining area for all children. Boys' Ranch/Girls' Town in Amarillo is big enough to have its own independent school district.

Some youth homes take in only children who have had no infractions with the law. Others will take children who have had such problems. Boys' Ranch/Girls' Town take such problem children. The main emphasis expressed by the people who run this home is that children should not feel like prisoners. A child who is sixteen or over and has had trouble with the law is not accepted. Children arriving there rapidly become pals with the children who are there. Once in a while, a newcomer might run off, but runaways are brought back. Children stay there until they graduate from high school. There is a remarkably high success rate. Out of 64 graduates at Boys' Ranch/Girls' Town in 1994, 28 received scholarships for college.

Boys' Ranch/Girls' Town has over 400 boys and 75 girls, hailing from twenty two states and from all ethnic backgrounds. Besides their schooling, they receive religious training and learn to work. Children at Boys' Ranch raise cattle, hogs, and chickens, and do some farming as well. From the time children are old enough to work, jobs are offered them in various endeavors. These include building new homes, milking cows, hauling feed, working in the laundry, and other tasks. For such work the children receive payment into an account they have at the Boys' Ranch Bank. These children can spend this money by writing checks for such desires as they have.

The homes at Boys' Ranch are not elaborate, but all serve a real purpose. They salvage children who could become state liabilities.

On our trip to Boy's Ranch, Mary King, the secretary of President Ted Lockey, guided us through the ranch. This was a very interesting visit for my wife, Manet, and me. The children we saw were all smiling, clean, and well groomed. The staff were very cordial and helpful. We visited several of the homes and were surprised at their cleanliness and the quality of their furnishings. The central dining hall where all the children eat at the same time was of the best quality, as was the elaborate kitchen. There were many other buildings on the property: laundry, schools, a church, swimming pool, vocational shop, and others. Besides pursuing schooling and work, the boys play football, baseball, and all other sports. There is a band and a choral group. The fine arts are taught. Boys' Ranch is indeed a fantastic facility.

We were reminded that these highly contented children were from broken homes, had left school, and many had been in trouble with the law. Manet and I conjectured what these children would be doing now, if it had not been for Boys' Ranch and they had been left to the elements, as they were prior to coming to Boys' Ranch.

Such homes that I checked have as many children as can be taken care of. Most requests for admission are turned away. If ample money were provided, such homes could absorb the vast majority of children who are in trouble or soon will be.

Society would well be served if children showing problems were to be sent to such a home instead of to jail. The important thing is to send a child to these homes before he or she "falls off." The children now at these homes were referred there by people who know of these facilities. Some families who have difficulties with a child and are able to pay for such a privilege do so. Indeed, it would cost society much less to send a child to a home like Boy's Ranch than it does for our juvenile department to handle such a child after getting in trouble with the law.

Today, there are so many children who are in need of good homes. Parent homes, with their limited resources, cannot begin to take care of such numbers. These homes operate very quietly, because they are besieged by people seeking such a home for their children. They are best known by their main source of revenue: people who contribute to these charitable institutions.

The best solution to society's problem of juvenile delinquency would be for our state governments to pass legislation authorizing payment to parent homes that desire to accept as many children as need a home. Any such legislation must be void of any attempt to tell parent homes how to operate their great humanitarian establishments. The respective boards of directors should remain in charge, with no strings attached. There is no doubt that the present capacity of these homes would be inadequate to care for all newcomers. Larger capacity would require the help of government funding. The cost would still be much less than juvenile courts, police, attorneys, jails, and prisons. Perhaps the greatest savings would be in the lives rescued from imprisonment and futures as adult criminals.

Children left in the care of a parent home have a much better future than those consigned to a boot camp or any other form of juvenile detention society has to offer. To expand the role of parent homes, we must determine who goes there, by what process, where, and for how long.

First, society must legally set up a process for making it legal and mandatory that children who are clearly out of control be sent to a parent home. CAB teachers will know and identify such children. Guardians of children who are going wrong will ask for help in placing their children. Society must okay the parent homes to be used for such children and agree to pay for such care. It should be the responsibility of the guardian, CAB teacher, and a juvenile department to make decisions as to which children should go to such a home.

Once a child is sent to such a facility, he/she should stay there until the parent home agrees the child has been set straight. Before such a child is allowed to leave, the juvenile department in the area of the child's home must agree that the child will be returning to a proper home life. If no such guarantee is forthcoming, that child should remain until high school graduation.

The homes I visited were very emphatic that children who are headed for trouble must be handled early. At Boys' Ranch, I was told that after sixteen a child who has gone astray has little chance of recovery. In some cases, children even much younger than sixteen may be turned down because the child is too steeped in problem ways.

Since 1939, Boys' Ranch has handled over 5,000 troubled children. Their experience shows that troubled children, in order to be reclaimed, must be removed from the surroundings in which their bad traits were picked up. For this reason, they advise that children should be sent some distance from their area of troubles. Some children find it difficult to adapt to well-adjusted surroundings, but once they make a few friends and get accustomed to good food, a good home, and peaceful surroundings, they change their attitude completely. They then show in many ways their appreciation for their new home.

Boys' Ranch founder Cal Farley preached the following:

"Give boys love, something to live for, a little recognition and the rest will take care of itself."

This axiom is still carried out by all who work at Boys' Ranch and Girls' Town; IT WORKS!

The essentials that Boys' Ranch and Girls' Town teach are as follows:

1. They are taught clean living, both personally and socially.
2. They are taught fair dealing and respect for the position and feelings of peers and adults.
3. They are taught to accept and carry through moral, religious, and social obligations.
4. Through training and instruction, children are helped to develop self-respect and confidence.
5. Academic and work skills prepare them for an opportunity for success in whatever college or occupational field they decide to pursue.
6. Most importantly, the children learn to accept responsibility, and are given every opportunity to learn to stand on their own feet and make their own way in life without having to worry about the stumbling blocks of ignorance.

CHAPTER 8

Special Problems of Our Black Youth

This is one chapter I hoped I would not have to write. However, I have such a deep concern over what is happening to our many black youths and their effect on our country that I could not walk away from this issue with a clear conscience without addressing it.

My concern stems from two sources. One is the great number of black children born to young black single women, many of whom are themselves practically children, and the destitute surroundings in which these new mothers must exist. The second source of foreboding is found in self-appointed black leaders who, for the sake of self-aggrandizement, mislead black youth to ignoble purposes.

As indicated in a previous chapter, I grew up on a dairy farm adjacent to the southeast corner of Oak Cliff, Texas. This area was populated mostly by black people, and I became acquainted with many of them. Some worked on my father's dairy. During the 1920s, my mother hired several black women to work in our home. When on errands, I frequently walked through areas where blacks lived in Oak Cliff. Never did it dawn on me that such areas were dangerous. Never did I see any young toughs out and about and up to mischief.

There were several churches in our area. On Sundays, these churches were full. Young black people, as well as their parents, were dressed in their finest. Religion played an important part in their lives, as did family life. Never was it evident to me that there were fatherless black children.

In 1935, I moved to Houston for a better economic future, and by the following year, I was on my way to building a wholesale grocery business. I pursued that career for fifty years. During this time I must have employed at least 5,000 black people, and I believe I learned to understand them well.

My company had annual year-end parties, at which time I presented profit-sharing certificates. These went over well. All our workers attended: black, white, executive, and blue-collar workers.

I was well acquainted with these people who worked for my company. The black as well as white employees were good family men who respected their wives and children. They were good, law-abiding citizens.

In the late 1960s, I detected a decline in the character of young black people at the same time their education was improving. The younger blacks started swapping wives or girl friends. Their commitment to work was not as it should have been, and job turnover was more frequent. They became more argumentative. We had to pass "no-fight," "no weapons," "no alcohol," and "no addictive drug" rules. As more Spanish-speaking workers entered our workforce, I found that they and our black workers often did not get along well.

I am still unsure of the reason for the change I saw in the black youth at that time. I believe, however, that even as their education improved, there may have been new influences being picked up at their schools. Some of these workers were coming from Texas Southern University, a black university, and the reader may well recall that the nation's universities were in political and social turmoil at the time. In addition, the new sexual revolution had begun.

As I see it, the difference in behavior among blacks, then and now, was brought about by several factors. First, there was the ever-expanding welfare system, which enabled ever-younger women to become mothers without the benefit of a husband. Second, there was the sexual revolution. Third, there was little or no responsibility on the part of absent fathers. Fourth, there were drugs. Fifth, there was the lack of education and/or training for available jobs.

It is inconceivable that the know-how in this country and the economic might that is available cannot correct the degeneration of so many of our black children.

I long ago concluded, from my association with black people, that the capacity for accomplishment is just as great in blacks as it is for whites. The problems of past generations manifested for blacks was inferior education, lack of opportunity in jobs, and difficulty in entering acceptable cultural and civic endeavors. All of this has changed.

Thanks to the NAACP, Martin Luther King Jr., and, of course, the many new laws that have resulted in the past thirty years, black have all the opportunities that could reasonably be hoped for. Today blacks in this country have the opportunity to reach whatever their goals may be. Indeed they are reaching heights never expected to be possible only a few years ago.

We have had a black woman president of a great university, the University of Houston. We have had a black chairman of our Joint Chiefs of Staff of our Armed

Services. We have had a black governor of a Southern state. We have a number of black congressmen and congresswomen. We have many black mayors and chiefs of police. Our president's cabinet has black members. There are many black judges, including one on the U.S. Supreme Court. Our athletic teams, in some areas, are dominated by blacks. With the tools now in place and with proper inspiration and hope, a black person who has the desire and ability can reach any height.

I should not leave out the factor that in business, too, blacks have been advancing rapidly. The June 1994 edition of *Black Enterprise* reports that for the year 1993 the BE100 broke the $10 billion barrier and got back into the task of job creation. With combined 1993 sales of $10.28 billion, the revenue growth of the BE100's was 13.9 percent of 1992. This group of businesses experienced their first major boost in employment, an incredible increase of 20 percent.

In November 1994, a very successful black business executive was appointed to become president of the giant Time Warner Corporation, effective February 1995. Time Warner is the huge media-entertainment entity whose business extends from publishing to music, movies, and cable TV. In December 1994, it was announced that Ruth Simmons, a black woman, vice-provost at Princeton University, would become president of Smith College, a 123-year-old, elite, private, Eastern school in Northampton, Massachusetts. Simmons is the daughter of a sharecropper. In September, 1995, Simmons assumed the presidency of Smith College. She was brought up in Houston's Fifth Ward, known as the Bloody Fifth.

The largest black-owned company, TLC Beatrice International Holdings, Inc., reported sales of $1.7 billion. TLC is a food processing company headquartered in New

York. Second in sales was Johnson Publishing Co. of Chicago with $294 million in revenue. Throughout the U.S. black enterprise is flourishing. Young people should be informed of the successes being reached by black people and encouraged to improve themselves.

Since World War II, blacks, who remained in school, lived clean lives, and aspired to succeed in business, politics, academia, science, medicine, or any other endeavor, have done so. Those who wished to follow politics and had the right message have found ample support from white boosters. The sky is the limit for blacks who really desire to get there. We now see blacks who have become scientists, educators, aviators, politicians, artists, lawyers, judges, and athletes.

Robert C. Newberry, a black columnist, reported in the October 8, 1994 issue of *The Houston Post* that in the past twelve years black households earning $50,000 plus more than doubled, topping more than 1 million. One-third of black households earned between $25,000 and $50,000 in 1990.

Mr. Newberry continues, "Sadly, government became addictive. Some blacks began thinking government could solve all their problems. Government assistance became handout-expectations instead of the safety net it was intended to be."

Mr. Newberry continues, "We see the failed policies all around us. Blacks have the highest percentage of single-parent homes, the highest percentage of teenage pregnancies, and the highest number of young males killing other young males of their own race.

"But then there are those who blame black-on-black crime on white racism. That's the ultimate cop-out for not accepting responsibility for one's action.

"Perhaps one day we will wake up to the need for all black people to take responsibility for what they do—and stop resorting to blaming other people."

President Abraham Lincoln declared freedom for black slaves by proclamation on January 1, 1863. But historically June 19th has been the date celebrated by blacks as their day of Liberty.

June 19th, as it is currently observed, seems to me a very poor reflection of what it should be, appearing to be only an occasion for drinking beer and eating watermelon. It should be a day of rejoicing in the freedom that was obtained, and one dedicated to helping fellow blacks who, though free, are bowed down in ghettoes and suffering while others have obtained an elevated station in life. To me, it would seem that once blacks have reached success, they would remember where they came from and reach back to pull their more unfortunate brothers from their distress. I see some such activity but not enough.

I have seen how ethnic groups help each other in this country, noting, for a number of years, how Chinese, Vietnamese, and Pakistani people helped their unfortunate brothers. Certainly, I have seen Jews help one another.

When you consider the great number of well-educated blacks in many areas of endeavor and the many successful black sports figures, there is plenty of influence and money to potentially be of great help in bringing other blacks out of the ghetto.

The great problem is that people mired in the ghettoes have lost hope, and instead of leadership and encouragement, we heap more money into this decay. Blacks with know-how throughout our land should form organizations dedicated to making contact with the unfortunate and bringing hope and encouragement that are so desperately needed. Every black gang member or lawbreaker, now so feared, was once a baby looking for someone in whom to trust, admire, and obey. Not having that person, he joined a gang where he thought he had friends. Civic groups dedicated to bringing a stop to the deplorable state of such children could do much. Educated black leaders who wish to help their people can devise the means and bring this about. Above all, they should advocate the institution of CAB education, which I feel would help black children more than any other.

The second concern I have for our black youth comes from the activities of Rev. Louis Farrakhan and his Nation of Islam colleagues. The Rev. Farrakhan is at his best when he addresses a gathering of black youths and tells them how to improve their lives. He tells them in very strong language to give up guns, give up alcohol, give up dope, quit helping to bring babies into this world and then deserting the mother, and quit killing one another. Indeed these are powerful messages that need to be told. If he and the other leaders of the Nation of Islam would stick to this mission, this organization would be a blessing for our black youth and our country.

The problem is that the Nation of Islam also has a mission that is not noble. The greater part of their efforts seems to be spreading divisiveness and hopelessness for these people. Telling these people how bad whites are, how bad Catholics are, how bad Jews are, and that they are being crushed by whites is of no aid and comfort for the more unfortunate of their listeners.

So that we can see just how serious the tactics used by the Nation of Islam are, I must quote some of the rhetoric that emanates from these people and answer it with facts. After analyzing these terrible audacious lies and misstatements made to students to whom these speeches are delivered, I hope you will find it easy to understand my concern.

The Nation of Islam preachers like to expound the fact that blacks were slaves in the United States and all blacks today should receive land and money for what was done to their forebears. Whites do not buy that. To such brazen demands, let us consider how some Americans might answer. Consider what the 40 million Americans, descendants of the Irish famines of the 1850s would think. Consider what the doctors, engineers, scientists, and business people whose forebears were known as Chinese "coolies" who helped build our Western railroads would think. Consider what the children of millions of European immigrants who arrived at our shores during the last part of the nineteenth century and first part of the twentieth century would think. Remember, my family arrived in 1913, having been mere serfs in Russia. All of the above-mentioned Americans have no guilt regarding slavery in America and dismiss such audacity for what it is—pure "Gimme." Black advocates who preach this way only succeed in making young blacks more confused and create for them false hopes. These would-be black leaders also succeed in further alienating whites who are sympathetic to black causes.

In November 1993, Khalil Abdul Muhammad, a member of the Nation of Islam gave a speech to the students at Kean College, New Jersey. In this speech he asked:

"Who are the slum lords in the black community? The so-called Jew. . . . Who is sucking our blood in the black community? A white imposter Arab and a white imposter Jew. Right in the black community, sucking our blood on a daily basis. . . .

"We can't even wear a ring or a bracelet or a necklace without calling it Jewelry. We say it real quick and call it jewelry, but it's not jewelry, it's Jew-elry, because

88

you're the rogue that's stealing all over the face of the earth.

"You see everybody always talk about Hitler exterminating six million Jews. . . . But don't nobody ever ask what did they do to Hitler? . . . They went in there, in Germany, the way they do everywhere they go, and they supplanted, the usurped, they turned around and a German, in his own country would almost have to go to a Jew to get money. They had undermined the very fabric of the society.

"Brother, I don't care who sits in the seat at the White House. You can believe that the Jews control that seat that they sit in from behind the scenes. They control the finance, and not only that, they influence the policy making."

(And so on and so on, with one sickening slur after another, all foul-mouthed garbage from an ignoramus.)

In April 1994, Khalid Abdul Muhammad was scheduled to address the students of the University of Toronto. But the Canadian immigration authorities took action to prevent Muhammad from entering Canada when it was learned that he had a prior criminal conviction of fraud in Georgia. Furthermore, they believed if he entered Canada he would violate Canada's laws against "hate propaganda."

Louis Farrakhan claimed on "20/20," the ABC television program, that the Nation of Islam was raised up to remedy the ills that have befallen the black population. I feel the Nation of Islam is to America what the Iranian-backed Hamas is to the Moslem nations rimming the Mediterranean Sea and Persian Gulf. They want to destroy any semblance of organized government.

On "20/20," Barbara Walters asked Farrakhan about the black youth involvement in crack. Farrakhan's answer was that the U.S. government introduced crack to blacks in 1985 to counter the black civil rights movement. Walters countered by telling Farrakhan that crack was introduced by illegal aliens well before 1985.

Asked about the illegitimacy rate of the many black children born to single mothers, Farrakhan blamed slavery. I know this to be untrue. I knew black people as a child. I knew them when I ran a business. They married and brought up their children properly in those days.

In short, Farrakhan simply likes to tell young blacks to "free themselves from the enemy—the white establishment."

There are educators in our universities who are in league with the teachings of the Nation of Islam. For instance, in July 1991, at the Empire State Black Arts and Cultural Festival, Professor Leonard Jeffries of the African-American Studies Department of CUNY charged that rich Jews helped finance the slave trade. He also claimed there was a conspiracy planned and programmed out of Hollywood, in which people named Greenberg and Weisberg and what not—Russian partners, the Mafia, put together a system for the destruction of black people.

Louis Farrakhan and his Nation of Islam preach that Jews were the slaveholders in the Southern states. Also, they claim that Jews were the people who brought the slaves to America. Let's examine the record.

During the period of the time that slaves were being shipped from Africa to America, Jews were scattered throughout the world. They had no power base from which to effect world commerce during the period of slavery. As for Jewish slaveholders in this country, the fact is the large slaveholders were on plantations in the South. (Very few Jews were plantation owners.)

Fact: Slavery has been carried on in the Arab world for over one thousand years. Slavery to the New World was initiated by Portugal, followed by England, France, and Spain. It is estimated about ten million slaves were extracted from western Africa to be sent to the new world. These people were captured at the direction of their Arab-Moslem masters and sold into bondage. The existence of slavery in Muslim society and by implication, the traffic in slaves, moreover, found sanction in the Koran and in the Shavi'a—the body of Islamic Law. Conversely, the Jewish Bible commands that slaves should be set free. Jews had themselves been slaves in Egypt for many generations.

Minister Farrakhan never misses a chance to ridicule white people in general for problems of black people, past and present. I would like to remind him that 359,000 white Northern soldiers died and 258,000 others sustained wounds in fighting to free black people during the Civil War. Also, I seriously wonder if Farrakhan really wishes his forebears had been left in eastern Africa to live. Perhaps he would now be living a more peaceful and less interesting life.

The Nation of Islam advocates are not the only people sowing seeds of dissension in our country. There are those who advocate violence. In our institutions of higher education, we have black educators who preach Afro-centrism and advocate the teaching of black culture, saying that blacks are mentally superior to whites. To prove this they point out that the Egyptians developed mathematics, built the pyramids, and so forth. Of course, they claim (on shaky evidence) that the Egyptians were black people.

Germans, Bohemians, Russians, Irish, Chinese, Japanese, and Jews all have cultures. I have never heard of any of these people ask for their culture to be taught in our schools. Peoples who wish to study their culture have done it on their own. Blacks should do as the rest of us did: Use the school to learn to be an educated citizen, law-abiding and capable of earning a living for oneself and one's family. After having done so, a person is at liberty to study on his own time. I was forty-five years of age before I felt I had the time to study my Bible cover to cover. Since then, I have studied many books of Jewish content.

On May 14, 1994, the retired former Chairman of the Joint Chiefs of Staff, Gen. Colin Powell addressed Howard University's graduating class. He told African-Americans they cannot afford "a detour into a swamp of hatred" and would break faith with their history to "show tolerance" for any philosophy based on ethnic or racial hatred.

Powell used this commencement address to respond to the recent furor at Howard over the speeches of Khalil Muhammad of the Nation of Islam, which have spurred a national debate over black-Jewish relations.

Powell said, "There is a great wisdom in the message of self-reliance, of education, of hard work and of the need to raise strong families. But there is utter foolishness, there is evil and there is danger in the message of hatred or of condoning violence, however cleverly the message is packaged. We must find nothing to stand up and cheer about or applaud in a message of racial or ethnic hatred."

Powell said, "As the world goes forward, we (blacks) cannot start going backwards. African-Americans have come too far, and we have too far yet to go, to take a detour into the swamp of hatred. . . . We as a people who have suffered so much from the hatred of others must not now show tolerance for any movement on philosophy that has as its core the hatred of Jews or the hatred of any other group."

In closing this chapter, I must include the prophetic words of Richard Nixon's final message to our nation:

"The greatest challenge America faces in the era beyond peace is to learn the art of national unity in the absence of war or some other explicit external threat. If we fail to meet that challenge, our diversity, long a source of strength, will become a destructive force.

"Our individuality, long our most distinctive characteristic, will be the seed of our collapse. Our freedom, long our most cherished possession, will exist only in the history books."

I believe this great American was addressing a festering problem, which must be resolved with typical American goodwill by all.

These United States are made up of a great assortment of individuals. These people came from many and all parts of the world. They are different in color; they spoke different languages when they arrived. Their talents, their customs, their understanding of morals, and many other factors are different. The vast differences are what makes us a great nation. The attributes of every one of many varieties of people have contributed to making the United States a great nation.

The downside of this amalgamation of these varieties of people comes from the few who do not wish to become immersed into the melting pot. Such people prefer to make for division of our people. I feel it is mostly for self-aggrandizement. Louis Farrakhan is a prime example.

We are at a time when the world is experiencing much racial, ethnic, and religious strife. We are experiencing much of these problems in our blessed country. Such violence as rocked Los Angeles in 1992 did great hurt to black people. Black leaders must know there is no winning by militancy or illegal acts. Militancy and aggression used when common sense calls for discussion and compromise can lead to disaster.

Let's hope that the Nation of Islam will listen to the real black leadership and drop its derisiveness, militancy, and name-calling. Such a change of direction could serve the black youth well. Furthermore, let's pray that the real leaders of black people; men and women of goodwill, understanding, and wisdom, will not fail to step forward, make their voices heard, and their leadership felt. In such an event and atmosphere, disadvantaged blacks will have a much better opportunity and avenue to advance from their unhappy ghettoes.

People of good will, civilized and desiring what is true and just for society, choose to explore, discuss, and reason. They do not harangue, accuse, and relentlessly vilify. Where people pick up clubs and use them as a means for advancement and settlement of differences, there is chaos. If we must look for examples, we can find plenty of such situations in Africa, where extremists and their religions lack the ethics and established way of settling differences that make Judeo-Christian morality, however fitfully, shine in the West.

As Ronald P. Bowers wrote in *The Houston Chronicle* of February 28, 1995, "The best and truest cultural development of American descendants of African slaves is right here. It is one of hard work despite little promise of success; pride despite degradation; honor and patience despite a natural anger against the injustices suffered; and a joy of great music, good food and wonderful humor.

"Such cultural virtues need to be recognized, emphasized and honored. No one need look to imaginary or mythical cultures of separatism when our shared cultural heritage is here to enjoy and be proud of while we work to overcome its failings."*

CHAPTER 9
The Bilingual Setback

I must now address what I consider a grave error Spanish-speaking people are making. Many are gung-ho in the effort to have their children taught in Spanish in our schools. The routine teaching of subjects to our children in a language foreign in America is certainly not of benefit to the young person entering the workforce to provide for himself. Any such person is at a disadvantage in the job market.

Over a period of fifty years, I employed at least 2,000 Mexican-Americans. My experience with these people left me with pity for those children who are taught in Spanish. The people I refer to had plenty of intelligence, but having been taught in Spanish only, they had to settle for the lesser-skill jobs—and of course earned the least. Jobs that required the study of a job description were simply beyond the comprehension of a man or woman who had not studied in English.

I directed my supervisors to locate evening schools that could help these people, but we never had anyone take advantage of the opportunity to enroll in an English course. It seemed that once students left school they were not inclined to return for further schooling.

Our country is falling behind the other industrial countries in education. The teaching of children in Spanish only is a prime example of our neglect for the future of these children and our country, as well. We are a great country because of the great wealth of the attributes offered us by the variety of peoples who have left other countries and came to the United States. Germans, Bohemians, Poles, Russians, Chinese, Japanese, Jews from everywhere, and many other nationals have made our country what it is today. Not one of these people ever advocated that their children be taught in the language spoken by their parents. Every child of such parents was afforded the opportunity to learn the common language that has made our country great.

Parents wishing to teach their children Spanish have every right to do so. But they should not place their child at a disadvantage by teaching him or her arithmetic, writing, history, etc., in Spanish. Teach him Spanish at home or secure a tutor at a time when the child is not at school. In Texas and all states that have a large population from Spanish-speaking countries, the high schools have very strong Spanish departments. After the children have been taught in English and have arrived at high school, they are thinking in English and should have no trouble in the job market. The proper time to study Spanish is in high school.

There is one more good reason we should insist upon all our citizens being taught in English. People who do not think in a common language will naturally withdraw from one another. A great country cannot afford to have such needless divisions. This is a sure way to destroy the fabric of our nation.

Anyone who begs to differ with this claim should take a trip to Quebec. Just go shopping in Quebec City or Montreal. You will quickly feel you are in France—not an English-speaking country, as we normally view Canada. To get this same sensation, you really do not have to leave the country. Take a trip to Miami and visit the areas now completely taken over by former Cubans.

The great increase of Spanish-speaking people in our country should make us apprehensive—especially when we consider such areas as sections of Miami, where English is now a foreign language. We should remember Canada, where a few years ago Quebec threatened to secede from Canada and the entire nation became a two-language country. We must take a good look at what is going on in the states that border Mexico. I hope we will avoid the fate of Canada. It is predicted that by 2020 half of the people in Texas will be of Spanish-speaking descent. How long after that will Texas possibly be threatening to secede? And join Mexico?

If anyone thinks the foregoing paragraph is preposterous, consider an article that appeared in the publication *Immigration,* a magazine published by the Federation for American Immigration Reform, in January 1995. This article says, in part:

"The hyphenated-American fad—Italian-American, African-American, Mexican-American—has taken a dangerous turn. What began as a way to combat prejudice and foster acceptance has become a call to create separate nation-states inside the United States. Irredentism, the formal name for the movement is gaining support in the Southwest as Hispanic nationalists call for a return to the land they claim was originally Mexico's.

"Hispanic lobby groups have promoted the idea lately to the return of Aztlan—the Chicano Nationalists' name for the Southwest—to Hispanics as a way to preserve their culture in America and fight discrimination in the Anglo's World. These same activists marched with Mexican flags through the streets of Los Angeles to protest Proposition 187."

Our country became great because all peoples regardless of race, ethnic background, or religion readily accepted the English language when entering this country and becoming a citizen. Many such newcomers retained and even taught their mother language to their children. I know of no people except Spanish-Americans who have refused to wholeheartedly accept English as the common language of communication.

Spanish-Americans are exerting great pressure on their politicians. They now demand all government affairs be conducted in Spanish as well as English. It would be a disaster for our society to be forced to operate in multiple languages. We must keep the United States one nation, indivisible—united by our common English. We must not allow ourselves to becoming a Tower of Babel. We must remain one country, one flag, one language.

The erosion of English is apparent in our public schools. Thanks to a Federal Bilingual Education Act passed in 1967, millions of children are taught in other languages—mostly Spanish—at a cost to taxpayers in 1993 of $226 million in federal funds alone. Add to this the cost state school systems suffer and you have spent big money. In September 1994, the American Legislative Exchange Council released a study funded by the U.S. English Foundation, which found that $12 billion is spent annually on bilingual education, with little overview for how the money is spent. And what are the results? We have children leaving school who are not qualified to hold good jobs; people who do not have good jobs often end up in poverty and crime. The crime rate of these people is twice that of whites.

The Supreme Court recently allowed a ruling to stand in the Spun Steak case, which guaranteed the private sector the right to require English on the job. The courts also threw out federal regulations used to harass businesses for having English guidelines. The courts said the Equal Employment Opportunity Commission (EEOC) had exceeded its authority in issuing the onerous regulations because Congress never gave this authority to the agency. The ethnic activists are not happy. They like the idea of forcing America's private sector to become bilingual. This further proves my point that it is wrong to teach pupils Spanish only throughout their school years.

U.S. Representative Toby Roth (R. Wis.) says America is rapidly becoming a society divided by language. He is chief sponsor of H.R. 739 a bill to make English the official language of the United States.

LULAC (League of Latin-American Citizens) is constantly pushing for more and more opportunity for the people it represents. One of the greatest things this organization can do for its people is to turn around the state and federal legislators. Legislators representing large Spanish-speaking territories generally push for bilingual schools. Of course, these politicians want votes first; what is really good for their people is secondary. It would be well for office holders to think of what is best for our country—not how many votes they get in the next election.

The most sophisticated Spanish-speaking parents are not in accord with bilingual education. They know what is best for their children. One Hispanic mother in Sun Valley, made five trips to the school her daughter attends before she got her out of a bilingual class. A foreman on a Texas ranch was dismayed with bilingual education, stating, "My children learn Spanish at school so they can be busboys and waiters. I teach them English at home so they can grow up to be doctors and lawyers."

Industry has its own problems. Because it cannot be

concerned about people who cannot do the job because of language difficulties, industry hires people who have educational skills to handle the skilled and better-paying jobs. The student educated in bilingual schooling has to settle for the lower-paying jobs. During the time I operated a wholesale grocery, I experienced several problems resulting from the fact that Hispanics wanted but were not qualified by lack of education for certain work. They filed complaints. Such cases are very costly to industry.

Spanish-Americans, as well as African-Americans, MUST accept the fact that in this country all possible laws and opportunities are now in place. If they wish to climb to success and reach new heights, they must get on the track that leads them to achieving such goals; it is the same track available to all people in this country.

Spanish-Americans, too, are succeeding. There are many examples. They are in Congress, in the President's cabinet and they are successful business people. Successful Spanish-Americans can do their people a big favor by pushing for the education of their children in an English-speaking environment. When their children graduate from high school, they will have much better prospects upon entering the job market. Certainly, they will have jobs better than washing dishes and digging ditches.

LULAC, for the first time, has elected a woman to be president of that organization. Her name is Belen Robles. Ms. Robles has an opportunity to achieve fame by getting her members to do all in their power to bring bilingual education to a halt. They can send a clear message to those would-be office-holders seeking LULAC's votes, to bring to a close this sad chapter in education.

CHAPTER 10

Controlled Substance Abuse and the Solution

On a popular TV show in July 1995, I heard a woman stand up and tell the moderator that dope was a good thing, because the selling of it produced jobs for young people who were poor. Most of us would dismiss this remark as an absurdity.

But for a moment, consider the viewpoint of impoverished children. They receive little guidance from good role models. Their clothes, food, and homes are catch-as-catch-can. Along comes the chance to make quick money and secure all those good things that will make a better life for them. Without a strong retardant in the form of a teacher, parent, or benefactor of some other kind, what will prevent these young people from joining the ranks of those who deal and use drugs?

Substance abuse is probably as great a contributor of the problems that beset our country as are the tragedies of children having children and single motherhood that contributes to our nation's poverty. Substance abuse brings about stealing, murder, rape, HIV/AIDS, the smashup of promising careers, and the destruction of those who become entangled in it. Many children are introduced to the sale and use of these terrible products every year.

The federal budget for fighting drugs has grown from $1.5 billion in 1981 to $14 billion in 1985, according to the annual report by Drug Strategies, a Washington-based police organization. If you count all the federal, state, and local spending in the past fifteen years, the war on drugs has cost $250 billion. The effort each year is more costly, yet we see little or no progress made in curbing the use of drugs. Those who are lucky enough to kick the habit sometimes give us the gory details. Often they claim they were introduced to these products before leaving high school—some as early as primary school. Once they are hooked, the habit becomes more and more difficult to quit. The need becomes more expensive, and in order to satisfy the need, no crime is too great in order to secure the funds necessary to satisfy the need.

Many of the users of these products share needles for administering these products intravenously and pass on diseases from one to another. Ultimately, society foots the bill in one way or another when these people can no longer take care of themselves and need medical attention. This has become a great burden to our taxpayers.

Our federal government has agents in the areas where controlled substances grow and are processed. We also have many law-enforcement personnel and equipment engaged in trying to prevent these products from reaching our cities. We spend money in an effort to have farmers in other lands grow products other than those that are manufactured into dope. All of this is for naught. The leaders of countries where these products are grown cannot or will not deny their farmers the opportunity to make a living off the growing of drug-related crops. The police of the countries through which these products flow cannot or will not halt drug shipments. Some arrests are occasionally made for show. South of our border, and most assuredly (to some extent) *at* our border, bribes ensure the dope cartels that their lucrative trade will go on.

There are over 2,000 miles of border between the U.S. and Mexico. There are 24 major ports of entry on this border. Thousands of trucks, mostly 10-wheelers, enter from Mexico every day. To inspect each of these trucks and their goods is impossible. At Laredo alone over 2,000 such heavily loaded trucks from Mexico enter the U.S. The inspectors try to check about 200 of these each day. To make the task easier, the inspectors inspect mostly the few empty trucks that come across. Along this border, there are only 1,620 inspectors and 244 dog handlers.

The objective of the U.S. Customs Department is to facilitate commerce. In the endeavor to make commerce flow with as little hindrance as possible, we are allowing controlled substances to be brought in as well. The drug smugglers are finding the gates at our entry points are made to order for their operations.

In addition to the truck traffic, 86 million passenger cars pass our Mexican ports of entry each year. Few of these are checked. When there is a back up of many cars at a crossing, the cars are waved through. Also, we must consider the thousands of ships and airplanes that travel from other countries to our shores and cities. On top of this, there is the revelation that our customs agents are being bribed to permit the passage of drugs.

Considering the above traffic with Mexico and other countries and the high profit in the drug operations, it is easy to see that there is no way we will ever interdict enough of the drug flow to ever control the ability of our citizens to secure drugs if they wish to acquire it.

Our law-enforcement establishment has become very capable of catching the distributors and sellers of drugs. They conduct drug busts and confiscate property and much money, which becomes an additional source of money with which to carry on our effort to slow down the drug trade. But there is so much drug traffic that our police are overwhelmed, and drug use continues unabated. The profit from the distribution and sale of these products is so great that it seems there are new young people lined up ready to take the place of those who are busted and taken out of the loop, so to speak.

Fully as much tragedy is brought about by drug use as from the use of firearms. But the sentences drug traffickers face when caught are too light considering the harm their products do. If we meted out commensurate punishment, we might get results. In Asian countries, where dope is not a problem, the problem has been solved by instituting the death penalty for drug trafficking. In China about two hundred people receive slugs in the back of the head each month for drug trafficking. In our country, while we continue to mete out ever-harsher sentences for drug trafficking, the profit in this trade has become so great I do not believe any degree of harshness will stop it.

So what are we to do? Should we legalize drugs, as some of our people advocate? After all, our experience with the outlawing of alcohol in the early part of our century taught us that as long as there is consumer demand for an outlawed product, there is a great profit in providing that product, and that there are no laws that can control the trafficking of such a product.

But as I see it, the user, who offers the high price to a trafficker to take chances in providing an outlawed product, is equally responsible for the crime of such provision. Society should accept this premise and cause the user to suffer some responsibility. When we look over the list of consequences from the use of controlled substances, we see that the user brings about a direct adverse effect upon himself, his family, his friends, and society. For users to go free, without any compulsion being placed on his errant behavior, is a cop-out by society. The least we can and should do is force a cure on any person discovered using such substances.

The U.S., with about 5 percent of the world's population, has approximately 2 percent of its citizens comsuming about 50 percent of the world's production of narcotics. If such people who wish to get their kicks would do so in the forests, in the mountains, or on deserts, that would probably be no one else's business. But these people, in order to get such substances, burgle, rob, or kill. They make themselves sick and give others their illnesses, including HIV. Women have babies born suffering with withdrawal from drugs. Mother and child create a great medical expense for society. The addicts fill our courts with criminal cases. Our jails and our prisons are overflowing because of them.

A recent study indicates the use of drugs by our youth is increasing. The only and sure solution to this problem is to forcefully "dry out" the youthful and other offenders promptly when they are discovered using such substance.

Some of our citizens, most assuredly the ACLU, will object to the use of law to prevent such usage. They should be ignored. We already make it illegal for our young people to use tobacco. The use of drugs is more harmful than is tobacco and each such user affects more people and society as a whole. There is no reason to delay our control of such substances by the method I advocate—stop the user from consuming drugs.

There are direct effects of drug usage as well as indirect effects. The indirect effects result from the vast profit the traffickers can make in providing the users with their dope and efforts by society to deter such activities.

Direct Effects:

1. Families are destroyed because one or more parents is a user. Children are left destitute as a result.
2. Drug-addicted women with little means bear children in public hospitals. The children are addicted. Society pays a high price to provide the service of delivery and detoxification of the damaged child.
3. Promising careers are destroyed.
4. Some die as a result of overdose.
5. In the marketplace, users perform poorly on the job. Their earning power is impaired. If discovered, they may lose their jobs.
6. Users cause accidents on their jobs. Society does much to prevent accidents in the transportation field, at great cost. (Some very costly accidents due to dope usage have occurred.)
7. Schoolchildren indulge in drugs, impairing their ability to study. Those in sports seem extremely vulnerable.
8. Users of drugs exchange needles and pass on AIDS and other diseases. Society picks up much of the great cost in treating these people.
9. Many abusers seek help to kick the habit. Those who can get enough money for this process do so. Of those who do not have the funds, only a few can be accommodated by society. The hard-core users die at a cost to society.
10. Tragically, there is no measurement for the great pain and suffering endured by the users and heaped on their families, friends, and children.

11. Great numbers of our robberies, hold-ups, and kill-ings are done by abusers in need of cash for the pur-chase of dope.

The Indirect Effects:

1. The cost of apprehending and prosecuting drug traf-fickers is tremendous.
2. Great outlays of money are necessary to cover the building of ever more prisons to hold the traffickers or users who have committed crimes. At least half the people in prisons are there for drug-related offenses.
3. The huge profits in drug trafficking bring about the bribing of the very officials charged with enforcing drug laws. This includes police, customs agents, fed-eral prosecutors, and even heads of state.

The drug traffickers can be stopped in their tracks if we go after the *users* as well as the sellers of these prod-ucts. Such a change would be cheaper, easier, and more successful. To do this we must once and for all embark on a dedicated effort to stop the use of these products. It can be done, if prosecuted boldly and with tough love.

We have in this country a number of treatment cen-ters for people who wish to get off drugs. Their track record indicates that users who wish to do so can be cured. This is an expensive procedure. But, when com-pared to the many dollars it costs to apprehend a drug pusher and still many more to bring him to trial and hold him in prison, it is a bargain.

It would cost very little to apprehend a user of dope and place him in a cure center. A simple test can show quickly if a person is using such a substance. When the test proves that a person has been using drugs, the pen-alty should be a one-way ticket to a treatment center.

Such centers could be private or government controlled. Experts in the field of curing addicts should decide how long individuals should be detained in such treatment centers while they are being freed of the habit. A person who has been successfully cured should be warned, when leaving, that if there is a next time, there will be a longer period of detention.

Instead of just worrying about the people who are trafficking in these substances, our police should then be looking for users, who are much easier to find. One method might be to set up "sting" operations to trap users. Employers should be encouraged to tell the police of suspected users. The greatest source of information regarding users should be found in family members. There is not a mother or father who would not be glad to have a drug-using child admitted to a treatment center. I am sure there are spouses who would be glad to have their loved ones go in for a cure also. I believe we would catch the young people well before they become hardened dopers, and while they could be easily cured.

At present, it is estimated we have two million users of drugs in our country. It is obvious that we have only enough facilities available to treat but a small portion of them. If we undertake the program I advocate, we would have to get ready immediately. Facilities for such a program could be found and/or made available with little cost. There are many old army camps available, and these would be inexpensive to refurbish.

The essential ingredient is to quickly train doctors and other caregivers to treat the unfortunate users, and to set priorities for their treatment. Of course, we should start with the young people who have recently embarked on this sad road. From all the information I have read, people who have reached their twenties without venturing into drug usage will probably not embark on this path.

In order for such a program to be successful, all successfully treated addicts must come out of the program in a state in which backsliding is unlikely, and such a degree that dealers are swiftly put out of business. Of course, addicts who are hardened with long years of abuse may be incapable of breaking free. These people would be the extreme, and it would be necessary to handle them differently. It might be best to have special facilities set up to give such addicts sufficient drugs to keep them functional, but not to have to make purchases from traffickers. Such a procedure is working well in England.

Facilities dedicated to the cure of addicts should permit few visitors, and these few must be scrutinized well enough to make sure no abusive substances are brought in. Caretakers must be carefully selected for good character. Visitors and caretakers should face stiff penalties if caught bringing in a controlled substance to the center.

The result of this proposed program would be a real success. Coupled with CAB schooling, young people would already be well informed of the consequences of embarking on drug usage. Parents, teachers, and the peers of these students would quickly know of any young person sliding toward becoming a drug user. This would lead to quick apprehension and the straightening out of such students. There would be such a preponderance of young people well trained in the need to abstain from controlled substances, that anyone trying to introduce drugs to students would be quickly apprehended.

There should be legal authorization for employers, owners of professional sports teams, governments, schools, transportation organizations, and any other concerns to test any employee suspected of substance abuse. Once a person is found to be using drugs, that person should have the option of voluntarily going to a treatment center or being sent by the government to such a place.

Such a program must be in keeping with a hospital-type of model, providing caring and treatment. It must not be set up with a prison setting. However, there must be a secure perimeter to prevent the possibility of anyone smuggling forbidden substances into the care center. A suitable board of review should see that no person is released until cured.

Something along these lines must definitely be done. As Andrea K. Walker wrote in a July issue of *The Boston Globe,* "Almost every American child—regardless of race, family structure or financial background—will be faced with the decision of whether to use illegal drugs before they graduate high school. . . ."* In the face of this, can we afford to do nothing?

---

* Used by permission.

CHAPTER 11

The Federal Government Dimension: From Hush Money to Seed Money

In the preceding chapters, I have pointed out many of the causes that have brought about the degradation of our youth. If we examine the sources from which come our errant youth, it is no surprise that the vast majority come from people living in poverty. Of course, we do frequently see the story of a juvenile from a well-to-do family who has gotten into trouble. But these are exceptional cases. The great number of juveniles whose names end up on a police blotter are no longer considered newsworthy. They are merely numbers added to our crime statistics.

A major source of America's trouble, poverty, should become the number-one project our country must resolve. If we do not, we are doomed; if we succeed, we can remain the world's dominant nation. As a nation we cannot fritter away the advances we have made for humanity. To default on our responsibility is inexcusable.

To explore the advance of poverty in our land, I have read and observed firsthand evidence, reports, and statistics. I have visited impoverished areas of Houston and Dallas that I was acquainted with fifty years ago. Today I find these areas in far worse shape than I remember. I see broken porches, broken windows, roofs in need of repair. I see unclean and unkempt children who, worst of all, look hungry and sickly. I am sure they do not eat regularly as did children fifty years ago. I can hardly describe the adults I see, many of whom seem to have lost hope and ambition, and look more like zombies than living souls. The only thing that keeps them alive and moving are government handouts. I will not address that issue, though, as stories related to it appear regularly in our newspapers and magazines. The story of such people as I have observed is not limited in locale to Houston and Dallas. I have seen the same thing in New Orleans, Los Angeles, and St. Louis. I am sure all Americans know it exists in every major city in our country.

It would be encouraging if what I describe had bottomed out and was turning around for the better. But the bottom is not in sight. If we go to areas where more affluent people live, we find that more and more fine homes are being built. I am reminded of my travels in Mexico and a few places in South America. There, the division of the poor and rich is quite apparent. At the present rate of the divergence that is occurring in our country, I am afraid we will too soon approach what can be seen in Mexico.

We must ask the question, "Why is it that juveniles from impoverished areas are prone to delinquency?" Of course, I have enumerated the many factors conducive to juvenile delinquency in previous chapters. The principal cause, however, stems from the fact that people of little means and no hope feel they have been robbed and cheated. They are angry and feel they have nothing to lose regardless of their actions. With such an attitude, they will do anything for money, feeling that even armed robbery and assault are justified. Many of our young killers are not the least bit remorseful.

Keith Bradsher, writing in *The New York Times* in April 1995, states that income disparity grows. New studies on the growing concentration of American wealth and income challenge a cherished part of the country's self-image. They show that rather than being an equalitarian society, the United States has become the most economically stratified of industrial nations.

Even class-stratified societies like that of Great Britain, which inherited large differences in income and wealth over many centuries, now have greater economic equality than the U.S. In truth, economic inequality has been on the rise in America since the 1970s. Federal Reserve figures from 1989, the most recent available, show that the wealthiest one percent of U.S. households—with net worth of at least $2.3 million each—owns nearly 40 percent of the nation's wealth. By contrast, the wealthiest one percent of the British population owns about 18 percent of the wealth there—down from 59 percent in 1920. Further down the scale, the top 20 percent of Americans—households worth $180,000 or more—have more than 80 percent of the country's wealth, a figure higher than in any other industrial nation.

"We are the most unequal industrialized country in terms of income and wealth, and we are growing more unequal faster than the other industrialized countries," said Edward N. Wolff, an economics professor at New York University. Margaret Weir, a senior fellow in government studies at the Brookings Institution, called the higher concentration of incomes and wealth "quite divisive," especially in a country where the political system requires so much campaign money. "It tilts the political system toward those who have resources," she said.

113

Let us examine the phenomenon that has brought about the ever increasing difference between our affluent citizens and those who are in poverty. I think Margaret Weir has placed the blame squarely where it belongs. Our great division of haves and have-nots arises from the fact that our economic rules have been established by the purchase of elective offices. And who buys those offices? It can be quickly and easily pointed out; people of wealth and power buy them. A prospective candidate for a seat in Congress must gather money to run for office, garnering an amount that continues to rise. For a run at Congress, a candidate must have millions of dollars. To gather such money, does a candidate for office go to the ghettoes or to the blue-collar districts for money? Of course not. He visits men of industry, professional people, men of finance, and any other people of means. In order to get the financial help he needs, he must agree to do those things that his contributors demand.

Once in office, the successful candidate has to vote for laws that he has obligated himself to support. As long as the office-holder does the voting against laws prejudicial to his financial supporters, he has an easy job of being reelected. Of course, once in office, congressional representatives and senators find it comes with a most attractive lifestyle, and they will do almost anything to stay in office. Also, once in office, these people go back home on occasion. And what do they do when they get back home? Do they visit the ghettoes and blue collar areas? Of course not. They ignore such places to visit the people who got them elected. They hold campaign rallies where they solicit money for their future campaigns. And who comes? You guessed it. The people who have been pleased with their votes and people who want certain laws passed and are willing to pay for it.

The Wall Street Journal dated September 7, 1995 had an article titled "The Best Congress Money Can Buy." by Albert Hunt.* Excerpts from this article follow:

Washington lobbyists are setting aside breakfast and cocktail hours this month and getting out their wallets.

Lawmakers representing districts all around the country are holding fund-raisers inside Washington's Beltway. For years the Democrats capitalized on this system, but now it's the Republicans, in the majority, who are taking most of the booty. More than three dozen House Republicans will shake the special interest money trees this month alone in the nation's capital.

The only change the Republicans have brought to special interest campaign contributions is that different interests are benefitting—the National Rifle Association and most industry associations are in, while the trial lawyers and most labor unions are out: Money, more than ever, talks. The GOP has taken the system, developed by Democrats, and expanded it to new horizons.

"There's no question the system is worse than ever," says Ellen Miller, the executive director of the Center for Responsive Politics, a nonpartisan group that monitors campaign financing. "In the past we could always track special interest favors; now it's happening so fast it's impossible to keep up." Overall, the Republicans are raising about twice as much in campaign funds as the Democrats this year.

The House Republican leadership is setting new benchmarks for aggressive shakedowns, and the followership is right in step. The 73 members of the freshman class—remember, the ones who were different, who eschewed the inside-the-Beltway stuff—are in the vanguard. In the first six months of this year, according to a

---

* Reprinted from *The Wall Street Journal.* September 7, 1995.

study by Common Cause, these newcomers raked in $11 million, almost half of it from political action committees.

The people who have contributed the big funds for a given candidate count that as an investment in the hope of laws advantageous to them. It does not stop there. Wealthy people and corporations hire lobbyists who will do whatever is possible to secure the votes in Congress that promulgate their hoped-for legislation. Still, this is not the only strategy used by the wealthy to secure the legislation that favors their causes. The newest thing is the soft money and Political Action Committee (PAC) money given to political parties, amounting to hundreds of thousands of dollars. Does anyone believe that such money is spent and no financial return is expected? Of course not. The process described here is one by which more and more "goodies" go to the affluent; and poor wage-earners be damned.

Our present political system has brought us to the point that we are on the verge of a calamity in our federal government. This situation is the reason for the ever-increasing poverty in our country. The people elected to fill our Congress and our Presidency are sworn to do what is good for our country. In practice, that is not what they do. The price of holding any of these offices is great, and so is the need to maintain a strong political party to support the seat; the name of the game has become "Smash The Other Party." It makes no difference how good a proposed legislation may be if proposed by a person of the opposite party; such a proposal is immediately denounced by members of the other party. Both parties play the game. I believe that, as a group, the members of the Democratic and Republican parties place the welfare of their respective parties ahead of that of the U.S. They would rather bash one another than contemplate, discuss, and compromise on needed legislation.

If our legislators spent less time fighting one another, many of our problems could be solved. For instance, our agricultural interests have to import thousands of illegals to work in the fields while we in the U. S. have thousands of people who need and cannot hold jobs. If the people on Capitol Hill would like to solve this situation, it could be done. Sanitary and decent work camps in our agricultural fields could be set up. People in need of work could be encouraged and transported to the work areas. The employers, denied the illegal workers, would be happy to have "legals" go to work. Our citizens may have to be paid a little more. The cost of produce may be slightly higher. But the results would be fantastic. People would be taken off the government dole and become reacquainted with earning a living.

While contemplating our tax structures, Congress should consider the cost of that dollar that finally gets to the unfortunates who are on any of our seventy-eight dole programs.

To begin with, it is conservatively estimated that the cost to American citizens and business is $200 billion just to comply with the bookkeeping and internal accounting necessitated by the Internal Revenue Service (IRS) laws. To that, must be added the cost of outside auditors and tax lawyers. The second highest cost is the tax paid to the IRS. The third cost is the IRS system with its vast number of buildings and workers. The fourth is the salaries and benefits for Washington lawmakers and assistants who make the laws for the needy. The fifth cost is the vast number of bureaus and overseers who dole out the money. Sixth is the interest the U.S. pays on money borrowed to give to the poor. It would be interesting to see what all of this costs our taxpayers. For one dollar to reach a needy person, I estimate that the cost to society must be three dollars. The Salvation Army provides money to the needy at a cost of eleven cents for every dollar of service rendered.

I can remember when there was no federal dole to help the needy. The local governments and generous citizens always took care of those in their midst who needed help. Local government and generous citizens still do so. If the federal government would get out of this business, I believe each state and city could again take care of the legitimate needs of our needy, but the federal tax system tends to preempt our ability to do so.

Another issue involves the great many of our factories that have gone over our borders. This is particularly interesting at this time, since Congress is looking into our federal income tax laws. At present, a manufacturer producing a product to sell in a foreign country has to look at the effect of income taxes to be paid if he is to be successful in selling a product overseas. That manufacturer must also think about how his stockholders will be rewarded in dividends if money is made. This is called, and is, double taxation, as the stockholder, too, will have to pay tax on the dividends. Other industrial countries do not have such a tax. Therefore, the U.S. manufacturer is at a disadvantage in pricing his goods to a foreign customer. Of course, this is a definite factor in whether or not a manufacturer stays here and how much he will pay his workers. Will Congress have time to factor into their deliberations of tax changes these concerns? No one knows. It depends on whether or not they will come up for air while bashing one another.

I believe the voter is getting fed up with the shenanigans—the dishonesty and ineffectual nature—of our two major parties. Both promise at election time to clean up their acts, but as soon as elected, they go back to their deceptive practices, feeling that they can fool most of the people all of the time. In 1992 Ross Perot scared both parties; Clinton benefitted. I believe if a man of Perot's standing were to mount a third-party campaign to elect a man like Colin Powell, money would pour in from citizens from all walks of life. These citizens would give generously to roust the self-serving Democrats and Republicans from office. More particularly, they would like to see an unbiased exponent of the American people in the White House. What this country needs is a leader for all the people. We do not need a leader who pushes the agenda for the Democratic Party, the Republican Party, or any other group. We need a leader in the White House who will listen to all the people and will cater to no group. Society has many problems to rectify, some resulting from unwise legislation. Let us consider the effects of some recent federal laws.

From the "*Time* Report" of October 12, 1994: The Census Bureau reports household income fell last year (1993) by $312 or one percent. Also, it reports that the number of families living in poverty increased by 1.3 million. Poverty is declared for families of four who live on less than $14,763 per year. This represents 15 percent of our population. Daniel H. Weinberg of the Census Bureau says, "The long-term trend in the U.S. has been toward increasing income inequality."

According to *The Index of Leading Cultural Indicators,* written by William Bennett: Of all children under the age of 16 who live with married parents, 12 percent live in poverty. For all children under 6 who live with only their mother, 66 percent live in poverty. In 1970,

10.4 million children lived in poverty; by 1991, that number had increased to 14.3 million. One child out of every five in the nation lives in poverty, and of all age groups, children are the most likely to be poor. Today, more than one child in eight is being raised on government welfare through the Aid to Families with Dependent Children (AFDC). During any month in 1991, an average of over 4.3 million families and 8.4 million children were dependent on AFDC.

The fact is that the effective income of hourly workers in this country has been declining for the past twenty-five years. Each administration and all the people on Capitol Hill like to tell the voters how they will make things better. We have ups and downs in our economy, but it made little difference the last twenty some years to many hourly workers.

In the lead article of the June 16, 1994 edition of *The Wall Street Journal,* it noted how poorly many people are faring on their hourly pay. These people work longer hours (both men and women) and have less to show for it. The trend continues—husband and wife work more and more hours, and their children receive less and less supervision. It does not take much imagination to see that families might disintegrate under such pressure; we have seen how that affects children.

Each administration likes to gloat over the improvement they have had on the economy during their period in office. It may be true that the overall domestic economy has improved and more people have been put on our payrolls in some given year. Upon analysis, though, we find that the real recipients of the better times are not the hourly wage-earners—the additional jobs are in fact going to service jobs made up of low to medium hourly wages. The good industrial wages are diminishing by going overseas. The fact is that each year hourly workers have been losing real earnings by seven-tenths of one percent annually since 1963. This means that families who depend on such income now have 20 percent less spending ability than they had in 1963.

On December 2, 1994, the jobless rate in the U.S. dropped to 5.6 percent—a four-year low. The Dow jumped 44.75 points. This was good news for people who owned stock. But if we looked at the average rate of pay for hourly workers, it meant little. The rate of pay for hourly paid workers dropped from $11.24 to $11.22 per hour during November 1994.

I do not subscribe to the theory that poor wages and poverty are the only problems that bring about conditions that promote juvenile delinquency. I have witnessed poor people, particularly blacks, during the late 1920s and 1930s, who remained good, law-abiding citizens. There are those today who think doling out money will cure lawlessness. I do not believe it will. I do, however, believe we should set the stage in our economic endeavors that will permit people to earn to the best of their capacity. Certainly we must agree that better income promotes family cohesiveness. Our government has failed miserably in promoting this necessary obligation. That significant and inexcusable dereliction of duty by our officials in Washington has succeeded in bringing down the earnings of our low-income and middle-class citizens. There are several contributing factors involved.

Parents who have little education, which often results in poor preparation for joining the job market, find their ability to make ends meet gets tougher with the passing years. A family with one parent who has had little education is particularly vulnerable. Children of such families are the ones most likely to become a problem to society.

The income of such families is greatly influenced by the minimum wage. That wage, $4.25 per hour, often means that children are left alone much of the time and may not be properly fed and clothed. That base affects the hourly rate of pay up the wage-scale to people making up to ten dollars and more per hour. If the base of $4.25 were higher, then the rates up the line would be higher.

In May 1995, the Labor Department reported that there are more than 4 million Americans working for minimum wage today—almost two-thirds of them adults. Seven million earn between $4.25 and $5.15 per hour. Many households depend on these wage-earners for the bulk of their income.

On May 2, 1995, Tufts University scientists reported poor children in America subsist on diets so nutritionally deficient that their ability to learn and become productive is jeopardized. The study found that one-third to one-half of impoverished children consume significantly less than the federally recommended amount of calories and key nutrients such as iron, zinc, and vitamins needed for normal growth. This translates to between one to four million poor children who do not get enough important nutrients to be healthy.

In July 1995, the Food Research and Action Center reported that four million kids are going hungry. Sixty percent of them live in households with at least one working adult. Of these households, 56 percent participated in the food stamp program, 25 percent were eligible but did not participate, and 19 percent were not eligible because the family earned too much money.

The present base of $4.25 per hour minimum was set by Congress in April 1991, over four years ago. During the interim our Congressmen have approved several healthy raises for themselves, while the economic health of low wage-earners has worsened with the passing years. Since April 1991, the income of the low wage-earners has, by my estimate, deteriorated about 14 percent.

The July 3, 1995 *Time* features a lengthy article titled "Working Harder, Getting Nowhere." The subtitle summarizes the essay's theme: "Millions of Americans hold two or three jobs, but still can't afford necessities and see little relief ahead." This article cites many examples of Americans who work hard and long and barely eke out a living. The article includes a portion of a report by the Labor Department, saying that despite the exuberant stock market and mild inflation, real wages keep falling. For the lowest earning 10 percent of workers, the weekly paycheck averaged $225 in 1994, a 10 percent drop since the late '70s, after inflation is taken into account. It means that more people than ever are working full time and still living below the poverty line of $15,141 for a family of four. "Millions more are scraping by, just one broken refrigerator away from a crisis." Labor Secretary Robert Reich says, "If we do not take steps to begin to reverse the trend for so many workers who are sinking in the new economy, we will be paying a high price as a society."

Congress also has in place Cost of Living Allowance (COLA) increases each year for Social Security recipients, retired government employees, and, of course, the huge pensions Congressmen get when they leave office. The minimum-wage people, however, get little if any sympathy from Congress. Why has Congress not adopted a COLA escalation for minimum-pay earners? (Remember $4.25 per hour for a person working 2,080 hours per year is $8,840. After deducting Social Security, it leaves a worker $8,209. I would like my readers to try to juggle a budget of this amount in order to enable a family of just three to live in a manner that any American should expect.)

If minimum wage and wages up to $10 per hour were regulated by supply and demand, I am quite sure people in such brackets would be receiving raises in accordance with the gradual decline in the value of our dollar. But Congress fails these people once again. I refer to the fact that our minimum wage looks so good to people in poor countries that they are crashing our borders with impunity. These immigrants, illegal or not, keep the wages of our less-equipped citizens from any chance of rising. They make sure the supply of workers content to earn $4.25 per hour is ever full.

On March 12, 1995, *The Houston Post* reported that the Social Security office issued about 6 million non-work Social Security cards. These cards are not to be used by people holding them for work in the United States. However, it has been reported by the Social Security Administration that employers have permitted about 2 million of such card-holders to work here. For some reason the Immigration and Naturalization Service has taken no action.

Several years ago, former Congresswoman Barbara Jordan was appointed to head a commission to study immigrant labor and come up with recommendations. Jordan completed the study and offered comprehensive recommendations in 1994. If adopted, these recommendations would be very helpful to our hourly workers. As of July 1995, no congressman has sponsored any of her recommendations. That month President Clinton asked Congress to lower the number of legal immigrants seeking work in our country by one-third, this being one of

Jordan's recommendations. Industry immediately responded very bitterly to this suggestion. The reason: Industry imports workers who take good American jobs for much less pay. Does anyone seriously believe that our well-paid Congress will concern itself about Americans who lose their jobs to imported workers?

According to *The Wall Street Journal* of November 28, 1994, 10 million legal and illegal immigrants came over our borders since 1980. This represents the third and largest wave of immigration we as a nation have experienced. Aided by recently extracted details from the 1990 census, analysts have mapped previously little-understood changes in immigration patterns across the country, shifts that cast doubts on the widely held view that immigration is always a net asset for the economy.

Also in the article, George Borjas, an economist at the University of California at San Diego, contends that the skill levels of these new Americans are headed in the wrong direction. "If we have learned anything from the 1980s, we have learned that there is more than ever a need for knowledge workers; yet, at the same time, we have an increasing pool of lower-skilled labor," Mr. Borjas writes.

Presidential candidates as well as congressional and senatorial candidates pledge to make life better for their constituents. You hear plenty of verbiage from our congressmen and presidents regarding the huge imports of goods from foreign countries and the detrimental effect on our wage earners. However, if we can believe the reports of our American news media, our Congress and presidents are failing our wage earners miserably. We are told our country is receiving goods manufactured in factories employing child labor, prison labor, and sweat shops. We have a negative balance of trade with practically every Asian country, nearly every one of which has thrown up restrictions to prevent our goods from entering their country. Why must our trade relations continue to be one-sided? It may not be difficult to understand if closely examined. To start with, the Japanese are reported to be spending millions of dollars every year lobbying our Congress. What other countries may do to influence our laws is probably not known.

If anyone thinks our presidents are immune from such influence, consider the fact that the year President Reagan left office he made two speeches at $1 million each in Japan. It was during Reagan's two terms that Japan had the greatest gain in the sale of their automobiles in our country and practically took over the sale of electronic devices here. At the same time this was occurring, our industry was hobbled by anti-trade laws that prevented our industry leaders from banding together to combat the deterioration of certain industries. As a result, high-income jobs were lost.

The Clinton Administration appears to be making a good-faith effort to change the negative trade balance, but I believe this president, too, will fail unless he adopts a tough attitude. I am reminded of an experience several years ago, during the early '80s, when some of our trade people pressed Japan to allow our rice and apples to be shipped to them. Japan's response was that they had to protect her farmers. What we needed at that time was a strong president who would say, "Fine, we will protect our auto and electronics workers." Had we done so, we would not now have the negative trade balance. The Asian countries, particularly Japan, have ingenious ways to keep our goods from being sold in their country. I am sure we could come up with a few tricks to keep their goods from selling in the U.S., if only the administration would permit.

The trade agreement signed in July 1995 with Japan, whereby our auto parts would find a more open market in the future, is in jeopardy. Japan is proving once more how it can consistently outsmart us. The negative trade balance to Asia continues to increase. Vietnam will soon join the other Asians in siphoning off jobs and shipping us goods that will result in a negative trade balance. We need to watch what effect the General Agreement on Tariffs and Trade (GATT), passed in December 1994, will have on our commerce. The North American Free Trade Agreement (NAFTA) is already seeing good jobs go to Mexico. These all affect poverty in our country.

In the past twenty years, many of our industrial giants have set up factories in Asian countries and shut out many good jobs in this country by closing U.S. plants. Of course, the cheaper-wage, manufactured goods come back to our shores for sale. The problem is the American worker who formerly built these products cannot now afford to buy them. Congress could do something about this loss of jobs, perhaps making it less appealing for our manufacturers to set up elsewhere.

Many of our business establishments in the last few years have resorted to two methods to reduce costs that have played havoc with millions of our workers. These methods, of course, are designed to lower labor costs. One of the ways is to go to labor pools for workers. Workers are constantly switched from one company to another, and thus cannot be certain of earning a regular wage. They are afforded no fringe benefits. Such people are denied any ability of ever securing a regular job and a career that has a chance of advancement. There are no vacations offered, no medical insurance, or any other benefits. Another trick used by many businesses is to employ many part-time workers. The effect is the same as labor-pool work. These practices are widespread and growing. I believe this type of employment is unfair. It is devastating to workers, many of whom work two, three, or even four jobs in order to get by. Such people, with children, cannot have a home life conducive to the proper care of children. If Congress is concerned about poverty, it will address and seek to alter these business practices, which doom people to poverty.

There is one other factor that has lowered the ability of our lower wage earners to keep up. That is, the advent of the electronic and computer age. We all admire and enjoy the comfort this age has brought us. However, this great advance has created such efficiency in industry that it has destroyed many jobs. It has also reduced the responsibility of many workers and brought about a decrease in wages.

The computer and electronic age has also had a disastrous effect on many entrepreneurs. Technology, for example, has enabled an office in any city of our country to operate establishments in any other part of the country. The effect has been the demise of many of our small businesses throughout our country. As a result, the income of affected business owners and their workers has been severely lowered. Many small towns have been reduced to few or no retail establishments. Chain-store establishments, with their cost-cutting methods, have learned how to operate with low-wage bases. While they advertise low prices, they have helped to produce more poverty wherever they operate. Many communities understand this and try to keep them out.

To summarize what our lawmakers can do for our low-wage earners:

1. Keep minimum wage in line with the cost of living. A big raise is overdue.
2. Prevent legal and illegal immigrants from taking our jobs.
3. Prevent industry from exporting jobs.
4. Regulate the import of goods from our trade countries in accordance with the treatment our goods receive when shipped to the same countries. Let us hope that GATT takes care of this, forbidding products from being shipped to our shores if coming from prison, child, and sweatshop labor.

In order to advance their own economic opportunities here, blacks, Chicanos, Asians, and any other group who feel they are not getting a "fair shake" should quit complaining that they are not being treated as equals by whites. Such complaints may make for stirring "sound bites" by minority office seekers, but it gets little sympathy from white voters. Every right-thinking American understands that people must earn enough to live. All people who are not earning enough to live properly should think straight and vote for office seekers they believe will seek to pass laws to improve the ability of low wage-earners to raise their income above the poverty level.

I read recently an account of someone who has formed an organization for low-income immigrants. I hope that person will open this organization to the purpose of helping *all* disadvantaged; black, white, Asians, and any others. The various trade organizations, the industrial giants, the legal profession, physicians, accountants, and nearly every other trade has an organization lobbying Congress. They do everything possible to elect politicians who will pass legislation favorable to themselves. But there is no organization looking out for the millions of people eking out an existence at $4.25 per hour. Any person who earns $7.00 per hour, works forty hours per week, and misses no time will earn only poverty-level income in a year. These people should unite to form one large organization transcending color, race, and religion. United, these people can gain attention and clout in Washington. In the meantime, we can be assured that the vast number of lobbying organizations in Washington will not work for legislation to help the poor.

Society deludes itself and pays a heavy price for permitting the continued low pay for millions of our citizens. The fruit of this system contributes heavily to neighborhood squalor, the breakup of families, juvenile, and crime. Our nation, long ago, saw the injustice of child labor and sweat shops and outlawed such conditions. It's time to outlaw poverty-level wages.

Any enhancement of the minimum-wage rate would raise the rates up the line for all people who are living in the poverty level. Allowance should be made for school-age and handicapped workers, with employers permitted to pay these people according to their productive ability.

Raising the earnings of the millions of people who work in grocery stores, restaurants, clerical, and the many other jobs could possible effect a small rise in the price of some products or services we purchase. However, the amount would be small. Having been in the grocery business for many years, I calculate that a half-cent to one-cent increase on each item sold in a grocery store could support a one-dollar-per hour raise for store workers earning six dollars or less per hour. This is not too high a price to pay for the good that would result.

Let's look at what enhancement in the income of the poorly paid would do. The payment of a living wage to people might help families buy health insurance and set aside a little money for a rainy day. Wouldn't it be nice if we could curtail the ever-increasing case load of our publicly supported hospitals, all because more families could afford health insurance? The greatest savings would come from the billions of dollars spent each year to fund the many programs our government supports, with billions of those dollars going directly into the pockets of bureaucrats.

Of course, many business owners will complain that a raise in the minimum wage will put them out of business. But that employer will not suffer any greater cost than would his competitor. Such complaints must be ignored.

Every employer has too many taxes to contend with. If he will analyze the problem, he will surely see the great amount of tax money necessitated by the cost of poverty. Every level of government shares in this tremendous cost.

In *The Houston Post* of October 8, 1993, Joseph Perkins wrote:

It was three decades ago that President Lyndon Johnson plunged America into its longest and costliest war—the War on Poverty.

The war rages on today, 29 years later. American taxpayers have contributed $5.1 trillion (and counting) toward the effort. Yet the Census Department tells us this week that there are more than 30 million poor folks in America.

So, then, after three decades of fighting poverty, the poverty rate remains unchanged. Somebody in Washington ought to raise a white flag.

131

The reason the government has so miserably failed to get the better of poverty is that the present welfare system concentrates almost exclusively on the symptoms instead of a cure.

Since the poor don't have much money, the government gives them cash, medical coverage, food stamps and job training programs—which don't get to the root cause of poverty: the breakdown of the American family. . . .

Between 1945 and 1965, when the government spent comparatively little on welfare programs, the American poverty rate declined from roughly 30 percent to 15 percent. Between 1965 and 1993—with welfare mushrooming—the poverty rate remained more or less constant at 15 percent. The costly lesson of the War on Poverty is this: It matters not how much money the government spends fighting poverty. Family structure has more to do with economic status than any other variable. . . .

Ultimately, the long-term cure and prevention of poverty, which eluded, lies with the family.

The government has spent the past 30 years subsidizing one-parent families, thereby perpetuating poverty. If government encouraged two-parent families in the same manner, we would finally see a meaningful dip in the poverty rate.*

The total number of welfare programs run by our government is seventy-eight. The cost to each American family averages $4,000 per year. If the wage earner of each poor family works 2,000 hours per year and you raised his earnings $2.00 per hour, his total earnings would be increased by $4,000 per year. This probably would eliminate poverty in 90 percent of our families currently living in poverty. Millions of mothers could then properly supervise their children. For the seven million families in trouble, it would cost society $28 billion, which

* JOSEPH PERKINS reprinted by permission of Newspaper Enterprise Association, Inc.

132

is much, much less than we are spending on these families. The savings would more than balance the federal budget. We would also lower billions from the state and local government taxes. If the government paid back to the employer a portion of the wage raise, we would still be far ahead. We should immediately raise our minimum wage by one dollar per hour and within one year step up the rate by one dollar more per hour.

The cost of governmental programs for the unfortunate goes up each year. We must bite the bullet. Half-hearted and token programs will not cure the ills that afflict us. Of all industrial nations, we have the highest percentage of people living in poverty. Doling out money has simply not worked. We must attack this problem like child labor and sweatshops were attacked a century ago. We must demand that industry and all employers pay people a living wage. We have conditioned low-paid people to become so docile that they live in little more than approved slavery. To do nothing and allow poverty to worsen each year will surely bring disaster upon us. We are, in fact, nearing that point today.

The rioting in Los Angeles in 1992 was described as a protest against the first Rodney King decision. But the fact is that the perpetrators were poor people of little means. Such people see little purpose in living a clean, moral, law-abiding life. They have nothing of value to protect or lose. If they see any possibility of gaining valuable goods for themselves, they will do so. All they need is an excuse. I hope our country moves rapidly to eliminate the explosive conditions that help bring civil disturbances to pass.

Congress is doing much talking, and so is our President, regarding the great cost of the many programs designed to help our poor. But we must stop the bread and

circuses we are doling out to our people. We have traf-
ficked in "hush money" for the poor long enough. Each
time a crisis arrives, we institute a new program. If we
now stop these programs without a substitute, we will
indeed have an explosion, perhaps along the lines of Los
Angeles in 1992. The alternative could be the hope of
better-paying jobs. People enrolled in our many programs
today are tired of standing in lines and tired of listening
to bureaucrats. They want their dignity back. They want
to say they are self-supporting and can take care of their
children. People who would rather take the dole than
earn $4.25 per hour will be better inclined to go to work
if they can earn a living wage.

During the 1994 congressional campaign, we heard
much from candidates about an overhaul of the various
welfare programs. After the elections, we heard the new
Speaker of the House, the new Majority Leader, and our
President all pushing for a tax cut for the middle class,
earners of $75,000 or thereabout. The welfare recipients
in the meantime are wondering what will happen to
them. No politician is saying a word about helping the
poor. They have no representation in Washington.

Before the elections, both major political parties
made noise about reducing the federal deficit. The Clinton Administration was stressing debt reduction. Part of
the Republicans' Contract with America concerned bal-
ancing the budget through a constitutional amendment.
As soon as the election was over, each side went into high
gear, trying to get the good will of the middle class, having forgotten what the election was all about. They were
now looking for votes for the 1996 election. What a spec-
tacle, with each side trying to buy off voters by promising
to lower taxes for the middle class! The bleeding of our
nation's fiscal affairs, the problems of our poor, and crime

were forgotten. The lawmakers are now working for deficit reduction. Our poor people are bracing for the shock that may befall them. I believe Congress should pass no laws designed to enrich the well-to-do people and companies at the expense of the low-wage earners. They should amend those laws that have brought about any such conditions.

The continued efforts of each party to buy votes surely is a contributing factor to the continued weakening of our nation. I think our country is ripe and ready for a Party of the United States, dedicated to the interests of our country and designed to stop the nonsensical conduct of our governing powers.

Americans! We must unite in a common effort! We must eliminate the great amount of poverty in our country! Not by expanding the government dole. Let's do it by paying people a living wage. Let's raise the hope and dignity of our people. Yes, it will cost a little more when we make purchases, but that increase will be a small fraction of what we pay in taxes for our government at all levels to take care of those people who are paid insufficient wages. It will make our country a safer and happier place to live.

CHAPTER 12

Cause for Action and a Call for Action

I have documented the ills of our nation in the previous chapters, discussing those societal maladies that may well destroy us, if left unattended, as we approach the twenty-first century. If we do nothing, our doom is sealed. But we need not be destroyed. The nations of the earth still look to us. We have everything going for us, except we have become complacent; we think something will come along to solve our problems; some magic force will solve our juvenile problems, crime, poverty, and our other ills. This will not happen. We must chart a course that we know is right and stick with it. We need a Paul Revere to wake us up. We need some Patrick Henrys to chart a course and a George Washington to get the job done. And each of us must be ready and willing to make sacrifices. We indeed have a war on our hands that is greater than any we have had in this century. This war is not in a foreign land. It's within our borders, within our states, within our cities.

The sacrifices I speak of include every one of us. It starts with our young children and teachers. School days and school years will have to be lengthened. Students and teachers will have to give more time to the process of learning, brought on by the need for teaching children how to live and respect others. The 80 percent of us who are financially well-off must be willing to pay for the privilege of bringing up all children in a way that will banish the shortcomings of our youths. We will also have to be willing to pay a little more for goods and services in order to wipe out the poverty and misery that exists in about 15 percent of our citizens. This situation contributes heavily to the delinquency of many children.

For over ten years, I have read of various methods tried by many of our city, state, federal governments, and school authorities to control the ever-increasing breakdown of our youth. Of course, along with the deterioration of our youth goes the ever-increasing crime. In spite of all the ingenious methods in effect, nothing has helped. The harsher the penalties become, the meaner the crimes become. Nothing seems to work. Now is the time; we can no longer delay the reestablishment of the ways that centuries of development have taught on how to civilize people. The method is simple and it is fail-proof: Every child must be shielded from evil ways and shown the right way every day from infancy through high school. We can accomplish this objective; we must not fail. Within fifteen years we can return to the ways we knew children behaved during the first half of this century. Where children are not properly taken care of by their families and they are prone to become a juvenile delinquent, such children must be taken away from such an environment and placed in surrogate parent homes. The cost is much less than jails and prisons.

The handling of such juveniles and older adolescents who have become criminals must continue as they are now handled. If children come under the influence of CAB teaching, there will be less and less juvenile delinquency and crime. I would hope for a spontaneous acceptance of such teaching. Teaching of such subjects as I have outlined in chapter 6, will most certainly have a powerful, good effect.

CAB teaching should bear down heavily on the sexual promiscuity that has come about in the past thirty years and is getting worse. Pregnant girls should be afforded no help unless the prospective father is identified. Once identified, the pregnant girl should be given that person's Social Security number. From the time that father leaves high school, he should help provide for such child. These Romeos know what they are doing; they should not be spared the hardship of the girl. A federal law should direct the Social Security Administration to provide that mother with the father's Social Security number, his whereabouts, and his earnings, anytime she requests it. The man's earnings should be subject to garnishment anytime he fails to meet his obligation as a father.

There are many fine organizations in our country. Many are social in nature. I hope every organization in our land that does not have a real service or community project will undertake such a project that will have improving poverty and juvenile behavior as its primary goal. To do so, such organizations should be prepared to help elect politicians who will carry out policies and laws that promote the proper upbringing of our children and prevention of poverty. The accent of politicians running for office on the theme of more prisons and tougher sentences for criminals has proved fruitless. Prevention and not harsh medicine should be our theme to the continued decadence of an ever-increasing number of our citizens.

Not only should organizations engage in politics to bring about better youth upbringing and reduce poverty, but such organizations should undertake, and if already so engaged, continue with the prodigious work being done by the thousands of organizations that are doing just that. I see billions of dollars going to such an effort. Of course, this shows that the Judeo-Christian moral of tithing is still alive and well in our land. If we add the billions of dollars our government taxes use for the aid of the unfortunate, our citizens contribute several tithes to such causes. If we all pitch in and do what this book suggests, I feel certain within a few years we could be spared much of this heavy taxation. Within ten years, the heavy taxes we pay because of poverty, crime, single mothers, and so forth will be reduced dramatically.

I was surprised recently to find that the Salvation Army is the largest organization dedicated to helping our unfortunate. Thanks to a December 1994 report in *The Wall Street Journal,* we now know that the Salvation Army in 1993 received well over $1 billion in donations. It surpasses the Red Cross in receipts and disbursements, operating at a cost of 11 percent. This means that 89 percent of the money this organization receives goes directly to people in need. No other large organization operates so efficiently. Certainly, our government cannot equal such efficiency.

Our citizens, through the many associations dedicated to helping children, could still be more helpful. We must get the attention of children, motivate them, and direct them to activities that will entertain and steer them away from gangs. For such purposes, school playgrounds and gyms should be open on those days that schools are not open. More playgrounds, if needed, should be available. Swimming pools should be open for children. All of these should be well supervised. Organized hiking, biking trips, and camping should be available during the warm-weather months. Citizens, more than ever before, should volunteer to make these and many other programs a success. We see plenty of our fathers and mothers doing yeoman service for their children who are involved in baseball, football, and basketball. We need citizens so involved that all children will have opportunities to participate in similar endeavors or interests that will point them in a proper direction: that are certainly directed away from gangs. Youth centers should be established in areas where there are many troubled youth.

Teenagers who need and want to earn money should be afforded the opportunity. I know many cities do all that is possible to secure jobs for such youth who wish to work. Businesses of all kinds should do all possible to create jobs for these teenagers. Minimum pay scales should be lowered for such workers. It may be preferable for our government to credit an employer for a portion of such a worker's salary. Guidelines should control the amount of time and the hours students can work.

The use of surrogate parent homes to straighten out children who have wandered onto the wrong track is a sure recipe for the control of delinquent children. I would hope all people and charitable organizations who have been blessed with the ability to give will contribute generously to such institutions. Surrogate parent homes are the best hope for the future of any child who has embarked on the road that leads to dishonesty, trouble, and crime.

Philanthropist Walter Annenberg, when announcing he was offering a half-billion dollars to be used for reforming public schools, said, "If this violence in our public schools continues it will not only erode our education, but will destroy the way of life in the United States."

Annenberg has appointed Dr. Vartan Gregorian, president of Brown University, to be his key adviser on how this vast sum of money will be used. I hope Dr. Gregorian will use some of this money to establish a CAB teaching program in a school district that has a great number of problem children. I hope all philanthropists will participate in helping school districts set up CAB programs. This additional financial help may be necessary, as school districts are always short of money and money restraints may long delay such implementation. I hope, however, that citizens will agree that CAB schooling will go far in curing the ills that bring on child delinquency. When citizens see real solutions and then let their officials forcefully know their thinking, action occurs. I hope that within two years we will see CAB schooling in many of our school districts that have the worst problems. Eventually all school districts, I hope, will establish such schooling.

Two of the biggest problems facing American society concern poverty and the ever-increasing supply of guns. Guns wind up in the hands of criminals and juveniles who don't yet understand such a devilish device. These two problems are both well understood by our citizens. Americans, by an overwhelming majority, are in favor of reducing or eliminating poverty. If it were not so, our governments at all levels would not be permitted to spend the hundreds of billions of dollars for the help of our unfortunate. Over 70 percent of our citizens have indicated a desire to take pistols out of the hands of people who do not need them. But, our lawmakers do not abide by our wishes. Let's explore what is going on.

With great effort, led by Sarah Brady, we saw the Brady Bill passed. This was a drop in the bucket compared to what is needed. We must have a federal law that will require handguns be registered to those who may have a need for such an instrument. Ownership must be afforded only to people who really have such need. The great number of pistols now held by people who have no need for them should be purchased by our government and melted down. Anyone wishing to keep a pistol as a souvenir could do so by rendering it unable to fire. Of course, after a certain period of time, any person, not licensed to have a pistol and found to possess one should be properly punished. The gun lobby—that group that pays off our federal lawmakers more than any other lobby—will have much to say about such a law. An over-whelming number of citizens would favor passage of such a law; it would save thousands of lives and much property each year. But the fact is that the elected representatives whom voters send to Capitol Hill get bought off by the gun lobby that works dollar magic with those officials. Note *The Wall Street Journal* article in chapter 11, page 115. For instance, we thought those dastardly automatic weapons that held large capacity magazines had been outlawed. We now find that such weapons were outlawed only by brand name. Now, the same weapons are being marketed under a different name; such subterfuge! How long will our citizens be thwarted by elected representa-tives who are for sale? We must once and for all tell those representatives to produce or we will send in someone who will. Such a law would not negate the right of a citizen to maintain a musket, a device with which we can fight an enemy with whom we are at war.

The Greek philosopher Aristotle said poverty is the parent of crime and revolution. The basic nature of people has not changed since Aristotle lived over twenty-three centuries ago. The poverty-stricken in our country are a factor in our ever-increasing crime. We must not wait until it leads to revolution. Much discussion is going on in Washington and elsewhere regarding the vast money we are spending on poverty in our cities. We dare not remove the "crutches" without offering some real permanent solutions. Not to give heed could bring us face to face with a real problem. Let us examine what is going on in Washington.

Shortly after the general election of 1994, the Clinton Administration talked about raising the minimum wage. No doubt this sounded good to the many millions of our workers who are enduring poverty at home. Along with poverty at home is the poverty and inadequate bringing up of children in those homes. Here again, we immediately could discern the lobby money flowing. The answer to a congressman who contemplated a bill to raise minimum wage, was another congressman's quick reply that such a bill would be DOA. Officials of several companies who thrive on low wages immediately made statements that such a bill was inflationary. Some business organizations issued reports stating that businesses would have to close. I heard of no lobbyist advocating a living wage for our poor.

Americans cannot put up with such excuses, and permit so great a number of our citizens to live in poverty. Once again, I wish to emphasize we are paying many, many more times for poverty to flourish in our midst, than it would cost if we paid above poverty wages. The people who live in poverty cost us much when they collect food stamps, seek free medical care at hospitals, and in many other ways. Of course, the worst part is that it contributes heavily to juvenile delinquency and crime. We must tell our lawmakers we want our people to earn living wages—so we can do away with all the government giveaways and much food-stamp graft.

Labor Secretary Robert Reich has identified certain industries as not wanting to pay the minimum wage and meet basic labor standards. He named garment, agriculture, restaurant, custodial, and construction industries as the worst offenders in hiring illegal immigrants. Reich said many of these industries are "running sweatshops that are magnets for illegal immigrants. We are developing Third World work sites populated by Third World Workers."

President Clinton has asked Congress to approve $1 billion in his 1996 budget to curb illegal immigration. Maria Echaveste, an official at the Labor Department, takes issue with those who say that people come to the U.S. for welfare and to have babies. She says they are coming here for work. This I agree with. The hiring of illegals is a violation of the law of the land. If our government really wanted to put a stop to all those illegals flocking over our borders, it could be done very quickly. All it would require is to scrutinize the hiring practices of the people employing the illegals. This would take far fewer people to enforce, and the results would be much better. I just do not understand how so many employers get away with hiring illegals. Many pay less than minimum wage. How much lobbying is going on to prevent the enforcement of the law designed to prevent working illegals?

In chapter 11, I covered the fact that there are seven million families in our country who exist on substandard wages. This costs our citizens in taxes and through contributions many billions of dollars. If our poor received at least poverty level income, we would be spared much of our children's delinquency and crime.

Many who oppose increasing the minimum wage say small business operators would be put out of business.

During the time I was in business, I supplied small business operators. I saw their hiring practices. Of course, many paid as low a wage as they could get by with. I saw more people pay a greater wage in order to get better people. This argument does not hold water. Small business operators, as well as big business operators, know it is important to have people at work who are interested, feel they are amply compensated, and are honest. Such operators know if their workers do not feel this way, the work will not be properly performed. Business people who treat their employees well are generally the most successful. Such business operators who pay only minimum wages must operate with his family workers only. I have seen these kind of operators. Workers stay one or two weeks and new ones come on. Such business operators should have no voice in establishing minimum wage.

There are those who say higher minimum wage is inflationary. The raising of minimum wage would indeed raise the wages of people who are living below poverty level. The people who receive these additional wages will, of course, spend it. These people are destitute; they will immediately put this additional money in circulation. Whatever product or service they produce will probably cost a little more. I believe every American would be glad to pay a little more for these purchases. Particularly is this true when we consider that our federal, state, and city taxes would be lowered because so many billions of our dollars go to the many programs, projects, judicial, and juvenile systems that result from the poverty-stricken. There are those who say increased wages would be too much for entry-level workers. I believe our school systems do not teach our high school graduates real work skills as do other industrial nations. And, of course, we have the many people who never graduate from high school. These people, I agree, do not deserve a higher minimum wage, but they must be put to work. Our papers are full of classified ads for people who have some skill. No doubt our places of work are requiring people with ever-increasing education and work training. If our elected officials on Capitol Hill would try, they could solve such a problem easily. The problem is that they would rather throw stones at one another. One answer is given in next paragraph.

We spend much money on trade schools. I have read many stories of how ineffective many of them are. The operators of many of these receive money and the students receive little. Such training could easily be transferred to the employer who is in need of a worker with a certain skill. The proposed method would involve the government remitting back to the employer a portion of the wages paid for a period of time while the new worker is on the job and is in training for the work to be done. For instance, if the minimum wage were six dollars per hour, the government for a period of time, (perhaps three or six months) would reimburse the employer two dollars per hour. The employer would have to train the individual as he works in order to receive the reimbursement. Certain requirements would have to be established with such an arrangement. The government would not participate for such a job enhancement more than three times. The government would not participate in helping such an entry-level worker more than three times.

There are several good accomplishments to be had by such a program. It can remove many unemployed people from the government rolls and into the many job positions that go unfilled every day. A large benefit would come from motivating people to work who are not normally in the habit of working because they have found they can get by just as well by working the government welfare programs. Workers who have never worked may well find joy in working. Also, they would be pleased to receive the opportunity to learn a skill. This would place worker training at the place of the job as required, at a much less cost than we now pay to send people to trade schools. We would also save in not having to pay unemployment compensation.

The remedies that I have documented in this book would do much for our country. A few of the benefits that are quickly attainable include:

1. Good teachers will remain on the job rather than quit.
2. Children wishing to learn can study better without interruption.
3. Children can go to school in safety and not be afraid.
4. Parents will not be sending children to private schools.
5. Killing and maiming by children will be eliminated.
6. Drug abuse, alcohol, and tobacco use by children could be greatly reduced, if not eliminated.
7. Children having children could be greatly reduced.
8. Raising the minimum wage could do much to reduce poverty for many of our homes. It would help keep husbands and wives together, thus keeping children in homes that have proven to be the backbone of good communities.

Some long-range improvements that would result include:

1. Reduction in robberies and killings.
2. Reduction in cost of security.

3. Reduction in cost of prisons.
4. Reduction in cost of juvenile police and justice.
5. Reduction in judicial criminal justice.

The United States has been the model of democracy throughout the world for most of this century. Our image has now been tarnished by crime and juvenile delinquency. Our citizens are on the move, the main motivator being a safe place to live. For many years we have heard of white flight to safer areas. We now see blacks who have met with success doing the same thing. I guess we could call that black flight. All of this must come to an end. We should have no such movement; wherever we live, we should feel safe and be proud of our neighborhoods. We must aim for such a condition to occur soon. Our country must remain a beacon for all nations.

In conclusion, I find it essential to share the following taken from the prayer book of the synagogue to which I belong, which has a page dedicated to the proper guidance of children. Perhaps we can all take heed of its message in order to shape and mold our future generation:

Children Learn What They Live

1. If a child lives with criticism, he learns to condemn.
2. If a child lives with hostility, he learns to fight.
3. If a child lives with fear, he learns to be apprehensive.
4. If a child lives with pity, he learns to feel sorry for himself.
5. If a child lives with ridicule, he learns to be shy.
6. If a child lives with jealousy, he learns to feel guilty.
BUT—

7. If a child lives with tolerance, he learns to be patient.
8. If a child lives with encouragement, he learns to be confident.
9. If a child lives with praise, he learns to be appreciative.
10. If a child lives with acceptance, he learns to love.
11. If a child lives with recognition, he learns it is good to have a goal.
12. If a child lives with approval, he learns to like himself.
13. If a child lives with honesty, he learns what truth is.
14. If a child lives with fairness, he learns justice.
15. If a child lives with security, he learns to have faith in himself and those above him.
16. If a child lives with friendliness, he learns the world is a nice place in which to live.